In Pursuit of Slow

In Pursuit of Slow

Stress less. Be happier. Accomplish more.

Jackie Jarvis

First published in 2017 by Thames House Publishing

Text Copyright © Jackie Jarvis, 2017

ISBN 978-1-909072-51-0

A CIP catalogue record for this book is available from the
British Library

Thames House Publishing
is an imprint of Harris Oxford Ltd
41 Cornmarket Street
Oxford, OX1 3HA, United Kingdom

Continue your Pursuit of Slow with Jackie Jarvis at

inpursuitofslow.com

PRELUDE

This book has important messages for you if . . .

You are running too fast, doing too much, and generally feeling disillusioned with the pressure to keep up.

Trying to be perfect can quickly turn into an ongoing battle. Your life becomes like *Groundhog Day*, more of the same, over and over again. You want to slow down but you won't give yourself permission. The race you find yourself in is getting harder to win. You are tired of the struggle. You want yourself back.

> *"Come with me where dreams are born and time is never planned"*
>
> Peter Pan

The saying, *'You teach best that which you most need to learn'*, is the reason this book exists. I have written it for myself as much as for you.

Learning lessons from the *Voice of Slow* is also my journey. *'Slow'* has been a word which I have been afraid of, a word which I have been running from all my life.

Running through time

I have been running for as long as I can remember. Pushing for things to happen. Juggling, multi-tasking, always trying extra hard to make things work in my life. The results have been varied. Like most people, I have had my ups and downs, but mostly I have kept going, often moving through life like a whirlwind.

I can remember when I was 10 years old, sitting on a swing in a local park, thinking about the passing of time. I remember saying to myself, I will remember this moment.

Swinging back and forth, shouting out loud . . . 'Soon I will be 15 . . . Soon I will be 20 . . .', and so on. At the time, being much older seemed so very far away. Looking back from where I am today, it does not.

I remember making a commitment to myself to always remember that time. To hold it in my mind, like a movie, so that I could replay it whenever I wanted.

I didn't know back then what was in store for me, which path I would take through life, and what I was here to learn. All I knew was that I was having fun and that was enough.

I do believe that before we are born, we choose the 'Play of Our Life', in which we are to be actors. We are given the adventure and the growth we need most in order to evolve. It is up to us to learn the lessons. If we fail to learn the lessons the first time, the same opportunity will be presented over and over again until we do. You may have noticed this in your own life; the same patterns keep reappearing in different ways, in different places, and with different people.

You take yourself with you wherever you go.

When I think back to the 10-year-old me, I don't really feel any different now. I am still looking out through the same eyes, it is just that those eyes now see things from an adult's perspective.

Time has passed quickly. Aged 10, being 50 (something!) years old seemed ancient, years and years away. Now I am here, it seems like yesterday that I was swinging on that swing in the park.

In Pursuit of . . .

I have always been *In Pursuit* of something since that moment on the swing. Something important that I thought I might find at school, by going to university, in my various relationships, through family and friendships, by visiting different countries, through my work, building a career, or by making money.

Whatever I was *In Pursuit* of has been elusive, at times hard to reach. Every setback was an opportunity to try again. To keep going. To keep pushing for more. To keep hope alive. To work harder, to look for another way, even when the way I chose happened to be blocked.

I was the only one who could do it. I was the one who held the key.

This is my journey in *Pursuit of Slow*. A path to greater enjoyment, life fulfilment, and peace. I want it to be yours too. The messages I have to share will enable you to:

- Feel the fear, but slow down anyway

- Give yourself permission to take a pause

- Be truer to yourself

- Have the courage to let go of, or change, that which no longer serves

- Find ways to reduce the stress and worry that blocks your happiness

To Trust in Slow

Ultimately, finding your own secret to being truly happy with yourself and where you find yourself in your life.

CONTENTS

How to get the most from this book

This book has been written from the heart and from my experiences in life – business and personal. In writing it I wanted to find a way of sharing the powerful messages from *The Voice of Slow,* which I connected with fully for the first time when I walked 900 miles on the ancient *Camino Frances* pilgrim route to Santiago de Compostela in 2015 and 2016.

Reflecting on my life and the paths it has taken, I realised that my own *Voice of Slow* has always been with me; I just wasn't giving it the attention it deserved.

As I share my journey through the chapters of this book it is my intention to take you with me.

I want to help you to hear your *Voice of Slow* so that you can stress less, be happier, and accomplish all that is important to you in your life.

Writing this book has had an ease about it that I have never felt before. At times, the words wrote themselves, and it felt as if I was being guided by a force greater than just me.

Read each chapter and allow whatever resonates for you to surface.

Do not judge it, just allow it to come forward.

Make notes about anything that feels significant. At the end of each chapter, you will find a special section with reflections from the *Voice of Slow*. These reflective questions will enable you to relate these powerful lessons to your life as you hear what your own *Voice of Slow* has to say to you.

Enjoy.

With much love,

Jackie

PS. You will find more information about me at the end of the book as well as, details about our In Pursuit of Slow Community.

1. The Voice of Slow

"The only tyrant I accept in this world is the still voice within"

Mahatma Gandhi

This chapter introduces the concept that we all have our own **Voice of Slow**.

Our *Voice of Slow* wants us to listen, to take heed. It wants us to stop running too fast and doing too much. It wants the best for us.

The conflict which often exists between our mind-based *Ego* and our feeling-based *Soul* is introduced here. This helps to explain what can impede our ability to slow down when required. Being open to listening to your *Voice of Slow* is the starting point in the process.

What does your *Voice of Slow* say when it whispers gently to you? Does it ask you to take your time, to stop juggling tasks, to stop pushing for more? Does it plead with you to rest for a while, to savour moments in your life, to take a pause?

Do you heed its calling, or do you choose to ignore its presence? Do you prefer to listen to another voice that speaks louder in your head, telling you that you can't stop, that if you do, you may never get going again? That you must not let anyone down, you must keep going?

Who says that you don't have permission to pause?

In quieter moments, you may hear your *Voice of Slow* calling and feel its presence. It wants you to be happy, to feel those moments of joy in your life, to be free of the chains that bind you to working so hard and continually pushing yourself. It wants you to know that you can trust yourself. You don't have to listen to 'shoulds', 'musts', 'must nots' and 'can'ts'. These are rules that no longer serve you.

The World Praises Fast

The challenge is that we are living in a society which applauds 'busyness'; we are all constantly in a rush, squeezing more tasks into already-packed agendas, multi-tasking, never having time to stop. Being busy can be interpreted as being successful; you may no longer be effective, you may not be happy or fulfilled, but if you are busy and accomplishing things, well, then you must be successful, mustn't you?

With modern technology, speed is everything. Fast food, same-day delivery, instant turnaround. Nobody can wait anymore. Our Souls often outpaced by the speed of the life which we have created for ourselves. Maybe this is why so many of us feel so out of balance and out of sync with our-selves?

Running too Fast, Pushing too Hard

As far as I can remember, I have always been *'pushing to make something happen'*, or climbing a *'metaphorical mountain'*. I remember overhearing my dad object to some-thing a school teacher had once said about me not being good enough to pass my 11+ exams and that I would proba-bly end up working in a supermarket (this was when I was only 8 years old!). These comments drove me to work harder than ever I needed to; I was probably the only 11-year-old to revise for the 11+ exams for three years! That work cycle has persisted ever since: despite getting to uni-versity and passing my exams I have always been pushing myself, over-doing the work required.

Couldn't stop just in case . . .

My obsession with work was compounded by my parents' divorce when I was 16 years old, which caused me consider-able emotional and financial hardship. I vowed never to let myself be left in the same position as my mother, and hence-forth, would never allow myself to rely on a man for any-thing! From that point on, I never felt like I had a safety net or a cushion to make my journey any easier.

Couldn't stop . . . had to keep pushing on . . .

This *'pushing'* has brought many good things into my life, but I have never really learned how to slow down.

When I was younger, I remember thinking that everything was very transitory, that what you did each day could be forgotten and renewed with something fresh the next day, that time was always passing, like the flow of a river, always moving.

When you rush, the river of time can seem to go faster, but when you slow down and pay attention to the flow, that same river can seem endless.

Why should you slow down though and pay more attention to the flow of the river?

What happens under Stress?

You may be familiar with the term *'fight or flight'* which describes the mechanism in the body that enables us to mobilise bursts of energy to cope with threats to our survival. This was same in prehistoric times as it is today, the only difference being our perception of stress. Fight or flight is an automatic bodily response when a threat is perceived and our autonomic nervous system puts our bodies on alert. Stress hormones are released, the heart beats more rapidly and breathing is quicker. However, the part of our brain which initiates this automatic fight or flight response cannot distinguish between a real or a perceived threat.

That means if we continually keep minds on *'stress alert'* and never let our foot off the accelerator, we can find ourselves dealing with perceived threats all day long! If we do not allow time for our bodies to recover from these stress alerts, we will eventually run out of energy. Also, the stress hormones created by these automatic responses are not good for our long-term health.

So, if you, like me, have been continually driven by fears of what might happen if you don't push, you can imagine what could end up happening to your stress levels.

So why not slow down – what stops you?

Why don't you sit by the riverbank and watch the river flow?

Fear Pressure

Much of the pressure we often find ourselves feeling is self-generated, created by our inner voices. Think of the voice that urges you to move quicker and achieve more, as your Ego talking, persuading you that you can't slow down. You have too much to do, you are too important, you must move quickly to achieve all your goals.

Think of the other quieter voice you hear as your Soul's voice This voice may have other plans for you, but can become drowned out by the noise and force of your Ego. At times, it can feel like you have two very different people influencing you, one on each shoulder, both vying for your attention.

What does your Ego say to prevent you slowing down? Are these statements familiar to you?

- If I slow down, will people think I can't cope?

- If I stop, no-one else is going to do this work

- I can't take time out, it is weak

- If I slow down, I may fail

- I have too much to do and it won't get done if I go slower

Upon hearing these messages, what do you do? Do you keep on going, drowning out the whisper of your Soul which implores you to stop and listen to what you really need?

Listen to your Voice of Slow

Think of your Ego as being the part of you (i.e. your mind) which has brought with it all the beliefs from your past. The opinions of teachers, parents, and employers, the voice that says to you loudly in your head, that you must keep going, that if you stop nobody else is going to do it for you. The part of you that lacks trust, that is afraid that everything will fall apart if you stop pushing. Your Ego is primarily driven by fear.

Your Soul, however, is the part of you that is driven by love and wants you to be true to yourself. The part of you that lies deep within and looks out through your eyes. It is the part of you that lives within your body and speaks the gentle words of slow to you. Your Soul has your happiness and joy at the forefront of its mind and wants you to question your fears of '*Slow*'.

Beliefs of your Ego v the Intention of your Soul

I have come to realise how my early beliefs were formed and it all now makes complete sense. I was doing what I could to protect myself from pain. From an early age, I was afraid of losing the security provided by my parents, so by the time they finally split up and my father had to leave, I had already prepared myself for it.

As a child, I was always planning, always active, always setting up things to do or to achieve. As soon as I was old enough to work I found a Saturday job and an evening job, then saved for a moped to make myself independent as quickly as possible. I never allowed myself the luxury of standing still, of doing nothing. The only problem is that if you learn to rely on yourself from an early age, it can make it harder later in life to trust anybody else and allow yourself to take your own foot off the accelerator.

In a way, I still feel like that child now . . . still planning, still setting things up, unable to stop.

So, if I were to say, right now, that I am unable to slow down because if I do, everything will fall apart and I will have nothing left . . . is that really true?

I know it is a strongly-held belief of mine, glued together with fear and hence very hard to shift. We now know that this belief is my Ego – my falsely-created, yet completely understandable thought process inherited from my past. My Soul, on the other hand, wants me to be happy and peaceful and knows that things can never fall apart. That if I slowed down I could be more effective, truer to myself, and would be able to help both myself and others more.

I couldn't stop though . . . I had to keep pushing on . . . ignoring the wisdom of my *Voice of Slow*.

I remember my Grandmother Peggy telling me to *'Slow down!'* Would I listen though? Would I heck! I often wonder if that is her speaking to me now as I write this book. The messages I hear, the things I notice that I didn't when she was alive; she was the one person in my life who never let me down, a constant loving presence I am truly grateful to have had in my life. We had a pact that when she died and passed over to spirit, she would contact me. Maybe this is her way of waking me up to my *Voice of Slow*. *'Slow Down Jackers!'* (The very words she used to say).

> *"Your Voice of Slow has something to say to you, something you need to hear"*

As I reflect upon this, I feel its truth. It momentarily loosens the hold that the beliefs of my fear-driven Ego have on me. Allow it to do the same for yours.

Reflections from the *Voice of Slow*

During this section allow your *Voice of Slow* to come forward

The *Voice of Slow* wants the best for you. It knows that you are enough, just as you are. Listen to its gentle voice and trust in its intentions.

A moment to pause

Just take a pause and sit somewhere quietly for a moment. Allow yourself to take three deep breaths. As you breathe out, let go of the tension you are holding in. Allow your shoulders to drop. Close your eyes and just sit in silence for a few minutes.

As you take this pause, let the thoughts that compete to take up space in your mind float past, like clouds in the sky. Let them go. Allow yourself this moment to reconnect.

Reflections

Without stopping to think, write down your answers to the following questions:

What do you believe could happen, in a positive way, if you slowed down?

What would not happen?

Which voice are you listening too? (your Ego or your Soul?)

Which voice would you like to listen to?

Now look at what you have written down and ask yourself the following questions:

What have you written down that is driven by or connected to FEAR?

What have you written down that is motivated by LOVE for yourself?

Your *Voice of Slow* will grow stronger as you read and respond to each chapter of this book.

2. Is Your Life Going Too Fast?

"The most difficult times for many of us are ones we give ourselves"

Pema Chadron

This chapter is about **self-awareness**.

If your life seems to be going by too quickly, then you could be in danger of missing out on important aspects. You may be striving, but never quite arriving, at the place to which you aspire. You may feel like something needs to change?

You do have the power to increase your 'daily happiness' if you are aware of the good things in your life whilst you have them.

Ask yourself

- Are you going too fast to remember the days as they pass? Are you spinning like a top, turning like a wheel, losing connection with how your life is supposed to be?

- Are you lost in your head, never truly present in the special moments of your life, missing the pleasure, always something to do, somewhere to be?

Speed v Slow

You may be comfortable with the way things are. Speed has become like an old friend that you are used to. You haven't got time for *'slow'*.

My friend said to me the other day, *'Jackie, I know I need to slow down but I am just too busy!'* Does that sound familiar? We laughed when she said it.

But why are we so busy . . . what causes our 'busyness'? What drives the speed at which we live our lives? So much to do, so little time . . .

I never noticed my life was going too fast, until I hit 50. Then it suddenly seemed to be going past way too quickly. Maybe it is because I am afraid of ageing. My nieces, who are now in their early teens, joke about my age, singing funny songs at each birthday, reminding me of how old I am. But I don't feel old at all.

Dreams

My nieces ride horses and are both excellent show jumpers. They attend large horse shows, jump clear rounds, and regularly win prizes. I often tell them that they are living the dream that I had when I was their age. They laugh when I tell them this. I wonder whether they realise how wonderful this moment in their lives is.

Sacrifice

Unlike my nieces, I didn't get what I truly wanted when I was younger, but when I was older I chased after my dreams like a mad woman. Nothing was as important as having a horse to ride, or fences to jump. I worked to ride – that was all that really mattered. I eventually found my special horse, had my time as a show jumper on the circuit, and loved every minute of it.

However, was it worth all the sacrifices I made along the way? Relationships that didn't last, the family I never had time to have, the world I closed my mind to, all because I just had to ride. The rushing around to fit everything in, riding early before work, shows at the weekend, always wanting to ride more, to do better. It was never enough though; I had one horse but what I really wanted was to be a full-time professional with a string of six horses. But that wasn't to be.

Important Moments

Now all that is over, but I still have the memories. I still ride my old horse Magic (she is 24 years old as I write this) in the countryside around where I live, enjoying these moments. I sometimes relive our best rounds of show jumping in my head, and I say thanks for every opportunity I have now to ride her as I never know whether it will be the last. Having damaged her tendons badly when she was 16 years old, I had come to terms with never riding her again, but by some miracle she got better. This was a similar feeling to the one I had when I collected my grandmother, Peggy, from the hospital when I thought she was never coming home again.

Something so wonderful that you couldn't have let yourself imagine what it could be like, just in case you were disappointed by the outcome.

If you have ever had a moment like this in your life, you will recognise this feeling: when something comes back to you which you thought you had lost forever, you value it so much more the second time round and are truly grateful for the chance to enjoy it again, to have it enrich your life.

Reversing Time

Time reversed for me when I was able to enjoy my old horse, Magic, once again. We are not flying round big courses at Hickstead or on the Spanish Sunshine Tour, but we are enjoying the peace and quiet of early morning rides up on the Ridgeway near where I live.

I keep her close by, she lives a simple life with a companion in a large field full of grass. It is a long way from the life she used to enjoy, stabled at a high-class private yard, travelling in a Mercedes lorry to shows, enjoying the best in horse feed, supplements, and aftercare. I used to spend more on her than I did on myself!

But now, when I take a moment just to watch her in the field after riding, I wonder whether she is happier as she is now. A relaxed life, with no pressure, and the freedom just to be happy with what she has got.

I know I am lucky to have been given the opportunity to enjoy a few quiet moments with my old horse. We missed out on a number of years together when she damaged her tendons, but I have this special time now, and in a funny way, maybe I too am happier than I was before.

So, when I find myself saying to myself, *'You haven't got time to ride?'*, or *'You haven't done your hours'*, I just ignore that voice and go!

Striving but never quite Arriving

You may have had something which you had always desired and are now striving for, a goal or possession, something which is now your main objective in life. The excitement and anticipation which you feel are good things.

However, maybe you can't wait to have this heart's desire? You want everything yesterday, and become frustrated with yourself, everyone around you, and anybody who gets in your way.

You hit the accelerator pedal and keep it firmly pressed down, vowing to keep on for as long as it takes. However, you start to forget the initial reason for your ambition, and the race to make it happen for yourself becomes a habit.

Your life becomes like a film on fast-forward, and you can't find the pause button.

All of a sudden, years have passed by and you are struggling to remember what happened.

- Are you yearning to press pause?

- Are you missing important moments?

Awareness of those Special Moments

My father, Roger – 'Rog' – who sadly lost his life to cancer at the age of only 69, was a master at recognising and relishing special moments. He had been an only child but made up for it by having five children himself; two from his first marriage (my younger sister Gillian and myself) and three from his second marriage (Marieke, Linda, and Robbie). Sadly, neither of his marriages worked out, but his relationships with both his mother and father, his children, and his friends all remained strong.

That was partly because of the time he spent nurturing them and the care he took over the little things. Rog always had time to pop into a charity shop to find a book that one of us might like and put it in the post; to cut out an article or something funny from the paper and send it over; to make a special trip for an event that mattered to somebody he cared about. He thought nothing of jumping in his car or on a plane to make sure he was there. This wasn't always easy as most of us lived in different countries, so it took a commitment to make these things happen. He made the effort and always gave you the impression that he had time, even when he had a busy, full-time career.

I do remember catching his eye at a simple family event in my grandmother Peggy's house when he could see she was having fun. He glanced at me with a nod and a wry smile which said to me without words, *'This is great isn't it?'* I knew exactly what he meant.

Now when I reflect on his life and the things that stand out . . . it is, in fact, these special simple moments, not the grand gestures. Rog gave of himself to people. He took time.

So, I encourage you to take time to see a friend you haven't seen for a while, to give somebody that matters some of your undivided attention. Do something just because you want to, not because you have to. There doesn't always have to be an agenda. Don't always be in too much of a rush.

Notice when something is just really great for no other reason than it just is!

Reflections from the *Voice of Slow*

Making the most of the Moments that Matter

During this section allow your *Voice of Slow* to come forward.

The *Voice of Slow* wants the best for you. It knows you are enough just as you are. Listen to its gentle voice and trust in its intentions.

Is there something on the horizon that really matters to you? Maybe a special event or the prospect of spending time with the people you love? You may be looking forward to it, but concerned that you haven't really got time. Your head may be elsewhere.

Why not take this time to enjoy it, to allow yourself to relish every second? Live the moments fully, as if they were the greatest gift given to enjoy for that day only.

Put everything else out of your mind. The only thing that matters is to give your full attention and time to enjoy this moment. Notice how you are feeling, and say a silent thank you for the opportunity.

Reflections

When are you going too fast?

When would you like to go slower?

What needs more attention in your life than you are giving?

What could you do differently?

Life passes by too fast when you are always in a rush – you need to slow down and savour the moments before they are gone forever.

3. What are you in Pursuit of?

"Give your thoughts a chance to settle down, then feel your mind clear like a still forest pool"

Buddha

This chapter is all about finding your real self by **slowing down**.

You can lose your way when you lose connection with your *'Why'*. Your *'Why'* is your purpose and your most important reason for what you do with your life.

Slowing down will help you to go forwards in a clearer, more inspired way, by knowing what to focus on and what makes you happy.

Taking time out to think will help you move forward at any stage in your life.

Ask yourself

- Are you happy?

- Do you know **why** you are doing **what** you are doing in your life, at work or at home?

Losing your 'Why'

I recently heard from a friend who has a successful corporate career, lives in a lovely big farmhouse, owns 2 horses, and enjoys a committed long-term relationship. However, she is unhappy. She hates her job and longs for a different life. The commitments that she and her partner have made to enlarge their property means that she can't stop working. She feels trapped, unhappy, and stressed. She is aware of the wonderful things in her life, but she doesn't have time to enjoy them, having to put in 80-hour weeks to keep hitting her targets. She has lost her *'Why'*.

I am sure this is a common situation to which most people out there can relate.

Working as a business coach, I have met many business owners who feel as if they have become trapped in their own businesses. They are not happy, but at the same time, they can't get out. For many, even taking a weekend off is almost impossible.

In these situations, it is very common to lose the motivation and the connection with *Why* they started their business in the first place. They are continually *in pursuit* but have forgotten *Why* and *What* it is all about.

Do you recognise this feeling yourself?

Fear v Love

Again, we come back to the Ego. How much does the devil sitting on your shoulder control what you are in pursuit of?

If you do not like where you are in your life right now, try exploring what you are not happy with.

Perhaps you don't like your job, or are in a relationship that isn't working or are involved with a business you want to exit but feel you can't. You are spending hours and hours of your life on something you are not happy with, the weeks, months and years pass by . . . but you are still there. You feel stressed and frustrated, not liking the situation you find yourself in but staying anyway, afraid to leave, but also afraid of what may happen to you if you stay.

You are not enjoying yourself anymore but don't know what to do about it.

If you ask yourself why you should stay rather than go, there will no doubt be many reasons that sound convincing. You might make excuses filled with lots of *'can'ts'* and *'shoulds'*, and it may frustrate you to talk about it.

You are probably *in Pursuit* of something that is no longer working for you.

Ask yourself how much of the reason you give to stay relates to the needs of your Ego. Be honest with yourself. Nobody but you is listening.

I have stayed in relationships for longer than I should because I was afraid of what others might think of me, or of losing my financial security, or feeling like I had failed.

I have given work situations and people endless time and energy despite knowing, deep down, that something was not right for me. I have been afraid to let go of situations in case it affected my credibility or my professional standing. I have spent large chunks of my life failing to make changes quickly enough, never really exploring what was going on, content to sweep any feelings of doubt under the carpet.

It is important to understand what you are in pursuit of; the longer you allow a negative situation to continue, the stronger the hold it will have over you.

The Mirror of your Life

We are all where we are in our lives for a reason. There is a saying I came across when walking the Camino which resonated strongly with me:

*"The ox would not know that
it was strong unless it had to
pull a cart"*

In other words, you will not know true happiness until you have experienced sadness. You have to have known pain to know pleasure.

If you find yourself in pursuit of something that you no longer desire, it may be because, in order to move on, you need to learn something from it.

I found it hard in the past to work with two particular business colleagues. One of them was very tough, insisting upon maintaining the rules and standards he was used to in his hard-driving corporate life. The other was a very focused and to-the-point Financial Director, who was both extremely challenging and very outspoken. I could probably not have picked two characters any more different from myself to work with!

I found their pace too fast and their way of communicating completely at odds with my own natural style. Despite recognising that they were both highly talented and capable of doing a good job, working with them was always hard work for me . . . and probably was for them too. We all tried our best, but nothing flowed smoothly. We might have lost what we were in *'Pursuit of'* together?

So, I kept asking myself questions such as *'Why am I here?'* *'What am I supposed to be learning?'* *'Should I give up, or should I stay and try and work it out?'* I was constantly torn between the various options. There were many reasons why I thought I should stay – there was all the hard work I'd already put in, the people I would have let down if I'd pulled out, and what I would lose in terms of professional standing. All this, coupled with self-doubt; maybe the situation was my fault? I just wasn't good enough?

When I look back, my original reason for being in *'Pursuit of'* this particular business venture was due to a strong vision and a purpose that connected very strongly with my core values. However, I was just not sure if it was the right situation for me. If it was a job, I might have considered handing in my notice, but it was a business venture and I was part of it. If you have ever found yourself in a similar situation, you will relate to this feeling of conflict.

One side says, *'Stay and work it out'*, the other says *'Life is too short and you should go'*.

So, I continued on, for just a little bit longer, waiting for a sign.

If you are not sure, wait. Do nothing for a while. Take a breath. There may be something to learn.

Negative situations are in your life for a reason

The other day I had another difficult telephone conversation with one of these business colleagues. He kept asking me to get to the point, becoming increasingly sharp with me, evoking uncomfortable feelings for somebody in *'Pursuit of Slow'*. After the call, I let out a big sigh and asked myself, *"Why am I in this situation?"*

The response to this question was interesting. I heard, *"Jackie, look in the mirror."* It then dawned on me. I realised that I often talked to myself like this, inside my own head, in exactly the same way that this person was talking to me. Over the years, I have not been gentle with myself. I have been sharp. I have hurried along, not giving myself time to think.

It was a big realisation for me. If I could learn to treat myself a bit better, if I could listen more to what the *Voice of Slow* had to say to me, then maybe I would no longer have to endure this type of communication in my life. Maybe this was the lesson I needed to learn here?

Hold up the mirror

If a similar situation exists in your life, hold up the mirror, and ask yourself whether what you are experiencing is actually a reflection of something you are doing to yourself.

We dislike things for a reason, and we feel uncomfortable for a reason. Maybe it is our Soul's way of getting the Ego to step aside. Give us enough pain and we will learn, and if we don't, the pain keeps coming back time and time again until we do.

It may need to get worse before it gets better

Sometimes you need to have reached your lowest point before it is possible to make your greatest breakthrough.

Things reach a crisis, you hit rock bottom, and only then do you admit to yourself what you really want and how things need to change. So, you reset your radar and unlock the universal energy which helps you to move forwards.

We can all get stuck, and lose our purpose or our *Why*; a cloudy vision, a flagging mojo . . . the longer it goes on, the worse it gets, until it suddenly hits a point where the pain is too great and we have to do something about it. We open up, we share how we feel about it, we take action – we want and need something to change.

What do you do when this happens?

One of my clients recently found themselves in this situation. Her industry had changed significantly and she was having to run faster and faster every day just to keep up. She and her business partner were losing staff, and they were both struggling to hold things together. My client was getting very tired and worn down. She was a wonderful, highly passionate, creative lady, but she was no longer using her true talents in the business. She was losing her flow and her reason for doing it; boredom had set it, and her mojo was at all-time low, which was negatively impacting upon the energy in the business. Everything was blocked.

She had lost the vision and purpose for what she was in pursuit of. She couldn't inspire the team because she couldn't inspire herself and consequently, tensions were developing between her and her business partner.

They all felt like they were racing towards nothing.

In Pursuit of Love

Having understood what had happened here, it was my role to guide them all to a better place, one where they could all reconnect with everything that really mattered. I needed to light the spark that was going to get the fire burning inside their business once more.

I set a task for the female director who was feeling the most disconnected. She had been saying that she had a vision but they just were not living it. I asked her to spend some time creating a montage of feeling-related pictures, a mood board, with phrases or sayings that expressed the vision and feeling she wanted in her business. I asked her to present it back to her fellow director, the HR manager, and myself at one of our sessions together.

Shift happens when you connect with your Soul's desire

What came back was nothing short of amazing. What she shared was full of humour and passion, with bucketloads of genuine Soul and authenticity. It instantly brought the business back to life and reconnected the partners. I could almost feel the energy shift as she was speaking.

This exercise was the start of a series of tasks designed to create alignment and buy-in from everyone in the business. We ended up having a very exciting session planning the way forward. I felt blessed to see this shift and delighted that something as simple as sharing something that really connected with the core values of the business owners had made such a big difference.

They now knew what they were *in pursuit* of. They had their dream back. Goals now meant something to them again.

They had gone from racing towards nothing and resenting it, to moving towards something meaningful, something bigger calling them to action. Their Souls came alive!

'Why' lights your Way

You must know what you are working for. When you lose that connection with your purpose, you can feel it in your bones, in your gut, and in your heart. You may try to hide it, but the signs are still there. You can't seem to get yourself going. You can't be bothered to take action. It is all too big an effort. You start complaining that things are wrong. You are not happy.

But when you connect with your *Why*, when you know what it is that you are striving for, then everything starts to flow. You jump out of bed with a purpose, you can't wait to get going, you look forward to every bit of work involved. It is an absolute joy.

You are in *Pursuit of Love*. A love of what you are doing and why you are doing it.

Why is at the core of everything in life. It is the silent force; we may not always be fully conscious of it, but it is always there, driving us on. The *'What'* and the *'How'* flow from this core *'Why'*.

My *'Why'* for *In Pursuit of Slow* is about fulfilling a desire to share. To share the insights and messages I have heard and continue to hear through the *Voice of Slow*.

Slow down to gain Clarity

To find your mojo again, you may need to slow down, take a step back, and get off the fast-moving conveyor belt. Stop for a while. Have the courage to stand still. You need to know why you have chosen this path and where it is taking you.

Life is too short to travel blind when you are blessed with eyes that can already see clearly.

As for me, I am grateful that I have been motivated to write this book. I feel the right things as I write. It is easy and it flows. I jump out of bed in the morning, looking forward to the few quiet hours I can spend on it before starting my busy day.

What do you feel strongly motivated to do and why? What is the driving force that ignites the passion in you?

You may have a contribution you want to make, a reason for doing something that makes sense to you. You may have been aware of it when you were younger and starting out in life, or it may have come to you later?

In Pursuit of what you want, not someone else's vision for you

Did you grow up in a supportive environment where you received strong career and lifestyle guidance? Or maybe you didn't receive any guidance and found yourself becoming lost and confused with your choices.

I had a strange situation when I was making my early career choices. I always loved English Literature at school. I loved analysing the characters and understanding the creative, expressive side of poetry. I didn't like subjects such as Mathematics, Economics, or Technical Drawing. However, when it came to making decisions about what university degree course to apply for, I promptly forgot my passions and thought only about what might lead to a good career and a good living. At 17 years old, I was already aware that I would have to find my own way financially in life and I couldn't waste time doing something I just enjoyed, it all had to lead to something. Many of my friends at the time received pressure or advice from their parents. I didn't. My parents had just broken up at that time and both were focused on putting their own lives back together.

The only thing I could think of that I was passionate about was the countryside. I wondered about a career in selling farms or country property. So, I researched courses with this in mind and found one called Estate Management. It sounded like it may lead to something along those lines . . . so I managed to get myself a place at Oxford Brookes University.

It was only when I was sitting in the induction day session that I realised that the course would be focusing on subjects that I didn't like and probably would not be very good at Valuation, Technical Drawing, Economics, Taxation, Law; what a huge mistake had I just made! So, I spent the next three years trying to force something into my brain for which I had no real connection or passion. Yes, I received a degree at the end of it, discovered I could learn things that I didn't particularly like, that I could pass exams and that I could stick something out. But did I want to make a career out of general practice surveying (yes, this was the course that I ended up taking . . . not much to do with countryside and farms, eh?) No, I did not!

So, I had to backtrack again to explore what I really wanted to do with my life. The panic of the need to earn a living still clouded my vision. I didn't know much back then about how to find out what you really do want to do with your life.

I was lucky in the sense that I had freedom of choice, but I was also rather clueless.

Getting unstuck

Many people find themselves stuck in a corporate career they don't like for years, all because it was expected and they just followed the path laid down by others, never questioning or challenging it.

My good friend Derek spent 40 years in a career in law because of the expectations of those around him. As a highly creative artist and sculptor, he was never well-suited to the legal profession, but he was clever enough to pass all his exams with flying colours, and so he carried on. It wasn't until he reached the age of 60, having seen his father and a very good friend of his pass away, that he suddenly decided he was done with law. He was going to do what made him happy, and he didn't care if he only had a very small amount of money to live on – other things in life were more important.

As soon as he had made that decision, his life changed. He went travelling for a while to clear his mind and refresh his Soul. By chance, he met a lovely Canadian lady, Wendy, and now lives most of the year in a cabin in Gros Morne National Park in Newfoundland, Canada. He has a large shed right next to the coast where he spends his days making his sculptures. He is happy.

This was a vision he had shared with me when he had previously been working as a legal consultant. He had lost his mojo and wanted out. He told me about his dreams of living in a cabin by the sea and having a shed where he could spend time exploring his passion for art. At the time, it was just a dream, but he put it out there and the universe answered. He had the courage to let go of something he was no longer in pursuit of.

It was from nothing that something could begin.

It is frightening to feel that what you were once in pursuit of is no longer giving your Soul what it needs to be happy. Not knowing what else you want can be a very scary place. It can be hard to walk away without something else to replace it.

The longer you wait, the harder it can be to take that leap. Derek waited until he was 60 to decide enough was enough. However, in many ways, this was perfect. Once he had made that decision everything seemed to align to reveal his dream before him. He didn't really have to try, it all happened for him. I often reflect on Derek's story.

Seeing your way clearly – Your vision

Your vision is your picture of what you want in your life. It is the film you play in your mind as you think about the future you want for yourself. It is good to dream, whatever age you are. A new vision can be created at any time. We are always evolving and growing, and what you think you might want as a 17-year-old versus what you want now may be very different.

There is a saying I came across recently which sums this up for me rather well:

> *"If I am still the same person*
> *at 50 years old as I was at 20*
> *years old, then I've just*
> *wasted 30 years of my life"*

Although we may still feel the inner part of us is the same, we will have grown both inside and out. There will probably be themes and threads that continue throughout our lives. Things that you have always connected with and always wanted in your life; experiences, feelings, responsibility, enjoyment and values.

Reflections from the *Voice of Slow*

During this section allow your *Voice of Slow* to come forward

The *Voice of Slow* wants the best for you. It knows you are enough, just as you are. Listen to this gentle voice and trust in its intentions.

Dare to dream

Think about what you want, how you want to feel and what your ideal life would be like. Make up a mood board – a montage of pictures and inspirational words. Put out what you want and look at it every day. Imagine yourself living this vision as if it were happening now.

This exercise is powerful. It is a starting point for many I work with in business. It can be easy to lose the picture of how you want something to be in the future when you are living how it is in the present.

Reflections

Take time out to give yourself some mental space.

Connect with this silent force.

Ask yourself "WHY?":

Why do you want to pursue your dream?

Why you want what you have created in your vision?

Why does it matter to you to live that vision?

Enjoying your pursuit

Whatever you are in pursuit of in your life, it is important to give yourself time to reflect and enjoy the journey. To enjoy the highlights and the joys. To take the learning from each situation that you must deal with *en route*. Days pass, weeks pass, years pass and you grow, older and wiser (hopefully).

There is something to learn from every experience, from each challenge, from each high and each low.

4. What do you say when you talk to yourself?

"The first point of wisdom is to discern what is false, the second is to know what is true"

Lactantius

This chapter is all about understanding how your **'self-talk'** impacts the way you feel.

By changing what you pay attention to, you have the power to change your *'self-talk'* to empower and enrich your life.

We explore two different voices and their respective impacts: the *Voice of Slow* and the *Voice of Urgency*.

By being conscious of the impact from these voices, you have the power to make the changes which will profoundly affect your well-being.

Ask yourself

- Are you aware that you talk to yourself?

- Do you hear more than one voice?

The Voices in your Head

If you hear voices in your head at some point, don't worry – you're not crazy! The words and the noises you hear are what is known as your internal dialogue. This is the internal chatter which goes on in your mind.

When I was younger, I used to enjoy comics. I used to imagine what life would be like if the thought bubbles used in cartoon strips were real if we could see what people were thinking.

We all have an inner voice which guides our choices and our actions. This inner voice can drive us on or slow us down; it has the power to influence almost every aspect of our lives.

Are you aware of your inner voice?

Beliefs influence Perception and Choices

Beliefs are thoughts which have been formed by experiences in our lives, influenced over time by parents, family members, teachers, friends, or bosses. It is these beliefs which represent the bedrock of how we now perceive life, work, and relationships. They are our guide in the dark. Our beliefs influence what the voice in our head says to us.

How many times as a child were you told to hurry up? How many times were you told that it was unacceptable to do nothing? Did you find yourself always expected to be active or achieving something all the time?

Are you aware of your beliefs about your use of time?

The Voice that urges you on

I often wonder where the voice which has urged me on all my life has come from – what beliefs does it have? This voice tells me that I must work hard if I am to achieve anything. It tells me that if I slow down or take a break, I may not succeed. It keeps me at my desk to finish just one more thing before allowing myself a break. The one that frightens me with *'lack'* if I don't keep going. The one that won't let me stop and change the way I do things.

What does the Voice which drives you say to you?

The voice that urges me on has been hard on me over the years. I have felt guilty for the breaks I have taken and only been able to relax when I have felt a sense of achievement. I have found it hard to give myself permission to slow down.

Working for yourself is hard when you have an inner voice which drives you on. You can only stop working when you have achieved something, and when you run your own business, there is always something to do!

The Two Voices

I often feel as if I have had two different people living inside my head. One speaks harshly and is tough on me. It tells me off if I don't get up early enough, or allow myself to get distracted without having finished off the items on my *'To Do'* list. This voice drives me on with fear: *'If you don't try harder Jackie, you may fail. You may have nothing, every-thing will fall apart.'* I dislike this voice and try to shut it out. I want the other voice instead.

The other voice is gentle, like a whisper in the wind. It tells me everything will be OK, that I am doing what I am sup-posed to be doing, that I can rest and allow things to flow from me. When that voice speaks inside my head, I instantly feel calm, I experience a sense of peace and am more com-fortable with myself.

I relate these two voices to the hard driving voice of my Ego and the softer gentle voice of my Soul.

If I allow the harsh voice (Ego) to take over, my mood changes to edgy, hurried, and irritable, which is crazy when you think about it. However, we are all guilty of doing this to ourselves, allowing our state and moods to be altered in an instant.

I have noticed how much I love being around calm, peaceful, easy-going people, and how uneasy I am around those with 'hard edges' who insist upon doing everything quickly. This could be a reflection of my two sides; the harder side driven by my pushy Ego and the softer side of my Soul.

It would be interesting to consider how much time and space I give to my Soul's voice on a typical day compared to that of my tougher Ego. Do I only allow my Soul to step for-ward after my Ego has had its say after I have pushed and exhausted myself to achieve everything I should accomplish during the day? Do I only allow it in when I feel I am ready? Could I allow it in more?

Once you become aware of the two different voices going on in your head and what they have to say to you, their power can be shifted. The Ego can loosen its grip. You always have a choice.

How do you talk to yourself?

In my experience, people who drive themselves by listening to their Ego voice set themselves high expectations, and more often than not, hold the same expectations for others.

They are usually hard taskmasters, who cannot wait for anything, who never praise or waste time on chit chat. They are not gentle on other people because they are not gentle on themselves.

You may recognise this Ego in yourself or others in your life.

The Tone of Voice – urging you on or allowing you to slow down

Listen for a moment to the tone of your own voice in your head, the one that gets you up in the morning. What does it sound like? Is it sharp or gentle? How does it motivate you to get out of that warm bed? Does it allow you to stay there for a few moments longer than you should? Or does it make you feel guilty if you have a lie-in?

The way you speak to yourself will affect your stress levels. If you always give yourself a hard time, it will be just like having a hard-driving corporate boss sitting on your shoulder.

If you are harsh with yourself, you will suffer in the end. Even if you tell yourself not to be stressed, your mind will still have to see and feel stress to be able to avoid it. If you tell yourself not to worry, you will worry anyway.

Don't think about a blue tree . . . don't do it . . . stop thinking about a blue tree.

The chances are that you now have a blue tree in your mind. It is the same principle with a thought, a voice, or a concern. If you tell yourself not to think about it, you inevitably end up doing so. The mind and the body respond in a similar way to both an imagined and a real event.

Think about something that really causes you stress. If you think about it for long enough, you can easily think yourself into a state of stress.

Now think about something that you really enjoy doing. Imagine yourself taking time out to do it. You deserve it. There is a kind voice talking to you. It is gentle, saying that all it wants is for you to be happy. That it is all OK and you can take this time just for you. You take a deep breath and feel relaxed.

The trick here is to learn to talk to yourself in the same way you might talk to someone about whom you really care.

To be gentle, kinder, more loving.

Allow your *Voice of Slow* in, the voice that wants you to be free, relaxed, calm, and to enjoy your life.

The Voice of Urgency

We create our own sense of time and urgency. Things that we feel we must have achieved by a certain time, and how we prioritise tasks. We are all different in how we deal with time.

- Do you have a sharp voice that commands you get going?

- Do you constantly tell yourself to hurry up?

- Are you a good timekeeper?

- Are you obsessed with time slots and agendas, even when you are not in the office?

Self-created urgency

To a certain extent, we create our own sets of rules and beliefs about what we should be doing with our time. Our work environment will no doubt have more structure than our private life.

'I never seem to have enough time', *'There are not enough hours in the day'*, *'I don't know where time has gone'*, *'Time is passing too quickly'*, *'I can't believe we are half way through another year already'* – these are all phrases which we hear a lot. I'm sure you'll catch yourself saying them to yourself from time to time; I know I do.

Nowadays, I make a conscious effort to get up earlier to extend my day and give myself more time to do the things that are important to me; my writing, exercise, being outdoors, reading, and just being silent. The rest of my day is already packed with interactions, talking, coaching, telephone calls, emails, social media, webinars, meetings etc. I need and I value that early morning time, just for me.

Perception of time

To animals and nature, time does not exist in the same way as it does to us humans, who live our lives by the clock, the structure of time enabling us to manage and make meaning of our lives.

The strange thing about time is that when you take the urgency or structure out of a situation and just let yourself be with whatever *'is'*, it brings with it a certain sense of peace.

You may allow yourself pockets of time like this when you go on holiday. The day just evolves. You eat when you are hungry, sleep when you are tired, and in between, you do whatever you feel like doing. This represents a break away from the normal urgency we all live with, the *'hurry sickness'* that can take over if we allow it to do so.

Reflections from the *Voice of Slow*

During this section allow your *Voice of Slow* to come forward

The *Voice of Slow* wants the best for you. It knows you are enough just as you are.

Take time to just become aware of how you are thinking and what the voices in your head are saying to you.

Once you are more aware of these voices, you have a choice. You can switch off the voice that is causing you stress, and you can give the one that wants you to be peaceful and happy the chance to be heard.

Challenging your beliefs

Take a piece of paper and write down the answers to these questions:

What do you believe to be true about slowing down?

Slowing down will mean I . . .

Is this your belief?

How does what you believe influence the way you live your life?

Is it what you want?

What do you want instead?

How will it benefit you?

What would you like the gentle *Voice of Slow* to say to you?

Imagine what it could be like if you took guidance from your own *Voice of Slow*?

Your *Voice of Slow* is always there, it just needs you to give it the space to be heard. Slowing down takes strength and trust. Slowing down may mean things can move forward in the right way for you.

5. Why run when you could walk?

*"Our patience will achieve
more than our force"*

Edmund Burke

This chapter is all about giving yourself **permission to slow down,** or to go at your own pace when needed – you always have a choice.

It is about making yourself aware of the negative aspects of rushing through life, asking yourself why you may be choosing to rush, and remembering that you can choose when to push and when to slow down.

Ask yourself

- Are you aware of the pace at which you are comfortable living your life?

- Are you aware of having a natural pace?

Your natural pace

We all have a natural pace which we feel most comfortable with. Think of it like the gears of a car. Some people always operate at top speed; they talk fast, move fast, and think fast. They can't seem to sit still for very long before they are up and about doing something. They can be exciting to be around . . . or exhausting! Others prefer to operate in first or second gear; they walk slowly, talk slowly, and appear to think more slowly. They can be peaceful to be around . . . or frustrating depending on your natural pace.

Those of us who are flexible enough to *'adjust their gears'* depending on what they are doing or who they are with, will always be the easiest people to be around.

I remember undertaking an exercise on an NLP course some years ago when we were asked to take a pen and tap out what we felt was our natural pace on the table. We were told to just pay attention to what felt right. It was like a message from the unconscious mind. When I tried, my natural pace was slower than I thought it would be, but as I tapped out the pace, I felt an immediate sense of calm.

Try it yourself.

I have found that I can go fast and I can go slow, but I am most comfortable at a medium, rhythmic pace.

When I rush to try and do too many things at once, I start to become ineffective. I have found working with two of my colleagues a challenge, as they both constantly operate in top gear. They have a habit of always hurrying me along in meetings as it is the pace they are both comfortable with. I have found this way of operating stressful and at times it has resulted in me feeling rather stupid and giving myself a hard time for not being able to keep up.

In different situations where the person (or people) I am meeting with, operates at a medium pace, similar to mine, everything seems to flow. My brain works perfectly and the outcomes are reached easily.

Do you recognise these differences in your life and the impact they have on you?

My mother is the type of person who always sticks to her pace. She is retired now and enjoys spending her days as she wants to, without the pressures and demands of a working life. She takes her time with everything and never pushes herself out of her own comfort zone. When I go to see her, I consciously slow myself down to match her pace. It is something I have learnt to do over the years, and whereas once I found her slow pace frustrating, I can now find it relaxing.

When I think back to my childhood my mother was always like this. She always went at her own pace and made choices based on what she felt comfortable with. If she ever felt under pressure in any way, she tended to become stressed and expressed how she felt accordingly. She found it hard to push herself out of her comfort zone.

A journey that started from early learning

As a child, I decided that I should always push myself out of my comfort zone. The problem was that this probably caused me to push myself more than I perhaps needed to, and more than I was comfortable with. As a child, I was always doing things, always trying to achieve something. My sister said she found me exhausting – I was always on the go whilst she was watched on from the sidelines!

I wonder what I was running from?

Upon reflection, I was probably desperately trying to avoid being like my mother. I feel a bit sorry saying this as she is a good person and I can see her better qualities now, but at the time, I wanted different things for myself in my life, I wanted to experience and achieve more. I wanted to live in an environment where there was less stress, where I could relax, one where there wouldn't always be the threat of an emotional outburst.

I did enjoy much of my childhood, but I was always slightly wary. I couldn't quite relax and go at a pace with which I might have felt more comfortable with. I made decisions about what to do with my life under pressure . . . pressure which I created for myself because of my perceptions of my mother's behaviour . . . instead of seeing her as being true to herself, I saw her as always being difficult and spoiling fun situations. She had her own demons that, at the time, I was not aware of. Nowadays I understand that much better.

Rushing through childhood

I always felt that it was down to me to make anything happen in my life. This is true for all of us, but I probably rushed my childhood so that I could be independent as quickly as possible. The problem was being young and naïve; I didn't always make the best decisions for myself.

Consequently, letting go and going with the flow felt like a big ask. You may relate to this at some level. Being aware of why you run when you could be more comfortable walking, is the first step towards greater awareness. Awareness gives you choices.

As I became more aware of the driving forces behind my unhealthy obsession with constantly pushing myself, it became easier and easier to let go. The more I did that, the better I felt inside. Things did still happen . . . in fact, they began happening more easily. I now pay attention. I look for new evidence that lets me know that it is OK to let go of the 'pushing' and relax with knowing that everything is as it should be. There is a lot of peace in that thought when you connect with it. Try it yourself just for a moment.

Why do we multi-task?

Why do we try to do too much at once? Instead of just concentrating on cooking our evening meal, we do the washing up, tidy away, write a shopping list, sweep the floor, water the plants and then wonder why the food we put on the stove has burnt (in my case anyway!)

Some people find the mere act of preparing a meal relaxing. It is physical and in some ways primitive. You use your hands and there is a sense of completion and satisfaction at the end of it. To do it well takes concentration.

Hence, doing too many things at once is likely to detract from the pleasure you could have gained from doing just one thing properly.

When my old horse Magic went lame, I had to hose her leg with water twice a day for a week for 20 minutes. At first, I tried to hook the hose up so I could do something else at the same time, but after struggling for a while, I decided that this was just too difficult, so I just held the hose and watched the water trickling down her leg. That was my task. I was helping my lovely old horse get better, so I just concentrated on it and sent her healing energy.

When I was finished, I felt relaxed, so I repeated the hosing twice a day for a week. I didn't try and do something at the same time. I just gave in to the task.

Try it the next time you find yourself attempting to multi-task, rather than giving one important task your full concentration. Stop yourself looking at your mobile phone in the middle of doing something, and give that one task all your energy and attention. You will find yourself feeling more relaxed and in tune with what you are doing.

Fast is not necessarily the best way

Going too fast means you are more likely to make mistakes and miss important things by rushing. When we constantly jump from one task to another without fully engaging, we end up burning more mental energy than if we had just given ourselves more time in the first place. You may relate to the feeling of exhaustion at the end of the day after you have been madly jumping from your emails, to writing a report, to answering questions, to attending a meeting, to making phone calls. And at the end of that day, what have you achieved? Often nothing has been completed in full, but you are still exhausted.

Days like this often seem to merge into one. When somebody asks you how you are, you say, *'very busy'*, but the thing is *'very busy'* doesn't always mean *'very effective'*.

If you find yourself operating in this manner, try to just stop, take a breath, and ask yourself 'What would I really feel good about completing by the end of the day today?' Allow yourself the time to concentrate on doing that one thing and work on it until you have finished. it. Notice how this feels.

It may not have been the quickest, but were you effective?

What is your work ethic?

We all have our own work ethic, a set of beliefs about how we should operate in work situations. You may be in a corporate role, self-employed, or part of a team running a smaller business, but whatever you do for a living, you will govern the way you work by a set of rules. These rules may have been explicitly created by your bosses, or by the company culture within which you now work, transferred over from an organisation where you worked in the past, or they may simply be your own internal set of rules representing your values or your upbringing.

I know people who have retired from corporate life and who have decided to work for themselves. They almost all found it extremely difficult to let go of the corporate rules they spent most of their working lives following. You see them doing the hours, writing endless reports, sticking to self-created deadlines, controlling themselves and others as if the boss is still watching over them. They are afraid to let go of a structure in case they can no longer function properly. The rules provide a wall of safety around them.

On the other hand, there are other people who lack drive and a purposeful work ethic, but who crave a support structure with some accountability that would give them a reason to get on with things.

So, what is your work ethic? What are the rules you set to get yourself going work-wise, be it for yourself, or for your company?

It is interesting to reflect on this, as it forms the bedrock of how we motivate ourselves and keep ourselves focused.

I know that I have a strong work ethic, having worked for myself since the age of 32. I have had plenty of practice at keeping myself going which hasn't always been easy. I haven't always spent my time wisely and I am sure there have been many, many hours and even years wasted on things that either haven't worked or upon which I have spent far too much time and effort because I just had to work hard and do my hours in the office.

I have learned that working hard is not necessarily the answer. It is about working well on the things that really are going to make a difference.

The signs of when to push

I had an interesting conversation the other day with a lady who described herself as an 'intuitive coach'. I was telling her about *'In Pursuit of Slow'*, a concept she could relate to. We started discussing the various causes of stress, and what can happen when you push yourself too much. She told me that she was an extremely driven person, but what she did was to look for signs so she knew **when** to push.

She operated from a place of self-awareness, going at a slow enough pace to be able to question herself, but with enough intuition to enable her to see the signs when they appeared before her.

I reflected on her comments that evening and realised that in the past I might have been running so fast, driven by fear of failure, that I kept missing the important signs that let me know where I should be pushing and where I shouldn't. I had been guilty of pushing myself harder than I needed to, just in case I didn't achieve something important down the line. I can think of many occasions when I have overruled my intuition, ignoring signs that suggested I was on the wrong path or course of action.

These days, I am much more aware of those signs, and by using the strong work ethic I have built up over the years, I am able to push and make the effort when the signs are there.

In Pursuit of Slow is one of those projects. I have seen and appreciated every single sign that has let me know it is exactly the right project on which to be spending hours of my time. It feels right, it has flowed, and it has been easy from the very beginning. The opportunities keep coming, and I have been brave enough to say *'yes'* to them, even when I haven't been quite ready with the final product: the live Oxford TV show, the PSA speaker competition, the Salus Women's charity talk; these all came along when I had only just launched *In Pursuit of Slow* and with less than 15,000 words of this book written. I said yes to all of them because they were signs that I was on the right track.

There have been other signs too. The person I ended up working with on the digital marketing side of this project has been perfect for me. Great team work at the just right pace. The comments and insights I have gained from listening to the many other busy business owner clients I have worked with over the years, have also encouraged me – they all need a bit more SLOW.

I listen to the messages I receive on a daily basis from my own *Voice of Slow*; they are always important. I look for the signs now and . . . guess what, I see and hear them! This has given me greater confidence and trust that *In Pursuit of Slow* will work and that I will get the chance to share these important messages with the world.

This has helped me to overcome the fears that have dogged me for years with previous projects, having invested hours and hours of time and effort on various projects, relying on others to put in as much effort as I was doing, only to find that at the end of the day, for whatever reason, the project didn't work.

I think I could write another book about what **not** to do! The thing is, that when I reflect upon these projects, there actually were signs at the outset for most of them that they may not have been the right thing to do. The most revealing point is how I was feeling about them at the time. I was feeling that I had to keep on pushing myself, not that I really wanted to. I was in *'driving it along'* mode as opposed to *'getting into the flow'*.

Maybe I was running when I could have been walking?

I was making it into a race to the finish line, as opposed to a journey where I was aware of where I was travelling and being able to enjoy every minute of it.

Listen to your body and what it has to say to you

When you are always running and never slow down, you do risk doing yourself damage. Just like a car that you run and run without ever taking for a service and will eventually break down. Illness and injury are nature's way of saying that if you don't slow down, we will do it for you! Many of the serious illnesses suffered by people I know have been preceded by periods of high stress.

I walked the *Camino Frances* in 2015, a 500-mile journey from Saint-Jean-Pied-de-Port in southern France to Santiago de Compostela in north-western Spain. Along the route, I met lots of very different people. On one particularly hard day, I started chatting to a lady called Alice who had been walking ahead of me. She had been walking very slowly and alone. She must have been in her late sixties. I wondered at the time how she would be able to manage such a long journey on her own, as she didn't look very capable of walking the distances. I had a few words with her as we walked along, and then we said goodbye; I didn't expect to see her again as my walking pace was far faster than hers. However, strangely, I did bump into her a number of times along the Camino when she checked into the same accommodation in the evening. She always got there but just took longer.

One day I asked her where she planned to end up the next day and her reply was *'I just listen to my body; it tells me how far I can go. When I need to, I stop. I have time, so I can take time.'* What a wonderful thought!

From then on, even though we didn't walk together, I often saw her resting under a tree, having a coffee, or popping into one of the many churches along the way. I always thought about her listening to her body. She was definitely listening to her *Voice of Slow* and was content to go at her own pace. She was not in competition with anyone.

She made it to the furthest end of the route, beyond Santiago, to Finisterre, the most westerly point in mainland Europe.

She always walked at her own pace, even though others practically ran past her.

Be kind to your body

Our body is the place where our Souls live, so we owe it to ourselves to look after it. We all know we are human and not machines, so taking care and valuing what we have is vital. If you have ever been ill or injured, you know how it feels to suddenly have what you once took for granted taken away from you, even if it is just for a short while.

When you are running too fast in life, doing too much, and not taking care of yourself, this is where you put yourself at risk.

Your body needs good nutrition, enough sleep (8 hours), fresh air and exercise. Be kind to it – it can't do its job of looking after your Soul if you don't look after it.

Reflections from the *Voice of Slow*

During this section allow your *Voice of Slow* to come forward

The *Voice of Slow* wants the best for you. It knows you are enough, just as you are. Listen to this gentle voice and trust in its intentions.

Take some time to ask yourself why you may be running when you could be walking in some areas of your life? Ponder some of the stories and examples this chapter; what is it that drives or pushes you along? Think about how comfortable you feel – are there aspects of your life where you are having to push yourself beyond where you are comfortable?

Reflections

Where are you running too fast in your life?

Are there times when you would get more pleasure out of something if you just slowed down?

What is your natural pace?

Are you aware of times when you are allowing yourself to maintain a pace that is out of sync with the way you are most comfortable and most effective?

How do you look after yourself?

Do you take care of your body and make sure that it can do the things you are asking it to do? Could you do more for yourself? If so what?

It is important to be true to your own pace, but with enough flexibility to up the gears as may be required in different situations or with different people. Notice when you are operating at a pace that suits you best and when you are moving out of your own comfortable pace.

6. What happens when you slow down?

"Climb the mountains and get their good tidings. Nature's peace will flow into you as sunshine flows into trees. The winds blow their own fresh-ness into you, while cares will drop off like autumn leaves"

John Muir

This chapter is all about understanding why it is so difficult for those of us who are used to pushing ourselves on a daily basis, at work and at home, to **give ourselves a break**.

Only once you can recognise what is stopping you from slowing down, can you begin to make the necessary changes.

Ask yourself

- Can you give yourself permission just to be?

Slowing down

Remember that feeling on holiday when you can finally relax completely, allowing yourself just to 'be', to potter without an agenda, to just do whatever you feel like doing? You can let go of your normal programme and rules. It is such a good feeling. And then what usually happens when you get back to work? It can be hard to get yourself going again, to switch back on.

I remember when I came back from walking 400 miles on the Portuguese Camino. I allowed myself to step away completely from my normal life for over three weeks; all I had to think about was to *'Walk, Eat, Sleep'* . . . repeatedly! It was difficult to imagine going back to work, force-feeding information into my brain, asking it to make difficult decisions. All I wanted was the simplicity of walking, just thinking about where I had to get to each day, appreciating my natural surroundings.

I felt like an alien from another planet when I returned home and entered my office for the first time to start dealing with *'work'* things!

Slowing down on the Camino had given me a taste of what it can be like when you allow yourself to live life simply. When you slow everything down. It was like going back to being like a native in many respects, moving from place to place every day. The challenge was to bring back the lessons and apply them to normal life.

Getting going again

So, it can be hard to get going again when you slow down; is this one of the main reasons why we can be afraid to slow down?

When you take a break, and go and do something completely different, you may have noticed that time does seem to naturally slow down. A week on holiday feels like a much longer time than a week at work because your brain focuses on new experiences rather than sticking to its usual unconscious habits. It is good for you to break these patterns of behaviours from time to time; by doing so, you gain different perspectives.

The fear of slowing down

Many people worry about slowing down. I know, because I have been one of them. Worries can be because of a belief that by admitting you want to go slower, you have failed in some way. Or it could be that you worry that by letting anyone know the 'pace' is too fast for you, you will be considered stupid or incapable? It could be that you fear falling behind if you don't keep up with the pace of others. I have experienced all these fears at different times and in different circumstances.

On the other hand, some people are so used to racing through life that they fear slowing down will mean they become bored, that their life will lack the stimulation they need to survive. For some people doing nothing for a week

is almost impossible. I know many high-flying business colleagues who fear going on holiday because they think that
they can't just do 'nothing'. I wonder why not?

Some people live their lives at breakneck speed because it
prevents them from thinking too much and questioning
what they are doing. If they did, then maybe they would
have to admit that everything was not quite right and once
admitted, they would not be able to hold things together in
the same way. So, instead, they just keep on doing more and
more.

Rushing and speeding through life can mask deeper psycho-
logical issues. In some cases, keeping busy acts as an anti-
depressant. This is OK, as long as it does not reach an unhealthy level and you fail to give yourself a break.

If you never truly free yourself up and allow yourself to go
slower in your life, you will never know how much you could
accomplish and how much happier you could be.

In the past, I have gone to great extremes to hold on to the
pressure, to keep doing. I remember going to look after my
mother after she had had a hip replacement operation. She
lives in a small house and space is at a premium. It was hard
for me to carry on with my work whilst looking after her in
her house. I really struggled with doing very little work for
a week. However, instead of just submitting to the task and
giving her my full attention, my head was half in 'I should
be working' mode. I remember my mother asking me why I
couldn't just give myself a break. I asked myself the same
question. I was scared of stopping, even just for a week.

Fear of delegation

I work with many people who are growing businesses. It can be tough for them as they expand and need to take on more and more tasks themselves, often things that they are not that good at because they can't afford to spend money on the extra resources or skill sets required. After a while, they get used to doing it all and find it hard to let go of these tasks and delegate even when they can afford to do so, fearing a loss of control. When it is your own business, being protective in this manner is perfectly normal, believing that you are the only one capable of doing everything.

A business owner admitted to me the other day that he just couldn't be the driver of the bus, the passengers, and the mechanic, all at the same time. He needed help to get to the destination. He recognised he couldn't grow a bigger business if he couldn't delegate.

Getting too used to the load you carry

If you continue to overload yourself, keep trying to go faster, or work longer hours to cope with the ever-increasing work burden, you will end up putting more and more pressure on yourself. The problem is that the heavier the load you carry, the harder it will be to be effective and accomplish everything you desire. This is where resentment creeps in.

Do you feel like the load you are carrying on your shoulders is at times too much?

What would it be like if you could delegate some of the load you are carrying?

Fear of 'letting' go to go slow

When I walked the Camino de Santiago, I had to carry all my belongings on my back in a rucksack. When I packed for my first trip, I completely overloaded myself. There were things that I just thought could not do without; make-up bag, extra clothes, gadgets, books, and bottles of stuff! I was afraid of letting go. The result was I found myself walking with a load so heavy that I found myself struggling to see the beauty of the places I was walking through.

It wasn't until I realised that having taken time out to walk the Camino to simplify my life, all I had done was to create an exact reflection of what was going on in my business life at the time. I was holding on to things that I really needed to let go of. I had got too used to the load I was carrying. It was only when I realised this, that I was able to do something about it. I ended up giving away all the things in my rucksack that were not absolutely essential to my journey. In fact, I gave most to an old man whose need was far greater than mine.

We all have things that can hold us back and make our journey through life heavy-going. You sometimes need to go slower to be able to recognise these things and to realise what may be holding you back.

What are you still holding on to that is getting in the way of you moving freely on your journey through life or in business? Is there anything in particular which is weighing you down?

What would it be like if you could simply let go? What is stopping you . . . fear of what would happen, or what you might lose if you did let go?

But think what you might gain?

Too many options

Sometimes, the huge number of options available to us in our lives can make decision-making far more difficult. With less choice, it is easier to focus. It could even be a case of asking yourself if you really need or want the thing that you were just about to purchase or the decision you were just about to make? By slowing down, you will have the opportunity to be more aware and this awareness creates an opening to either do something different or, to do nothing at all.

Being afraid to focus solely on one thing

I think back to the number of balls I have juggled in my business life, the number of opportunities I have created for myself, the different hats I have had to put on or take off. All because I was afraid of fully committing to one thing. Maybe I didn't have the conviction or confidence in myself or in the thing that I was doing at the time?

What I do know, is that the number of options I had to keep open at all times was exhausting! I kept switching my focus from one to the other, with nothing ever getting my full and complete attention. I wanted to see the signs that something was going to work before I made it the 'front-runner option'. The problem was that because nothing ever received my full attention and focus, nothing ever stood out!

Are you able to focus in your life or are you spreading yourself too thin?

When you do slow down, you allow yourself a chance to properly explore your options and to decide what might be the best one to focus on, rather than juggling everything at once.

Distractions from being alone with ourselves

Today, our high-tech lives mean that we are never alone. Most of us have a mobile phone or a tablet by our side on a continual basis. Our lives are filled with communication and information. Technology naturally speeds things up. We always have some form of distraction from ourselves available.

The younger generation has never known it any different. Six and seven-year-olds (and often younger!) sit glued to games on phones or tablets when years ago, they would have been making up stories or playing hide and seek. Technology affects our ability to just to 'be' with ourselves. The word SLOW to many is a dirty word. We live in a society that is being taught that FAST is always better than SLOW.

The effect of this way of living over time will make it difficult to people to remember how to go slow – continuous distractions and interruptions will become the new norm.

When my two lovely nieces came to visit me in the summer, they would sit in the lounge both watching their own programmes on their iPad, or texting on their phones. Gone were the days of simply sitting around talking, or just enjoying a book. There just seems to be too much distraction. I hardly ever see someone just sitting doing nothing at all.

Is it hard for you to just sit and do nothing? What happens when you do?

Connecting with the silence of your Soul

I go to a regular meditation class as I recognise the value of being guided to pay attention, in a different way, to myself. By that, I mean my inner self, as opposed to my external self; the inner part of me that wants to be silent and still. When I arrive at the class straight from work, it often takes a while to clear my mind of the thoughts that jostle and crowd it. Others at my class have said they feel the same. We need that sense of doing it together, of having allocated the time to focus on ourselves without distractions, to spend a few hours enriching ourselves as our leader guides us to our inner selves.

The feeling I get when I finally manage to allow the internal chatter and random thoughts to float away and connect with the great silence and peace beyond is worth the 'letting go'. I always feel better afterwards. A sense of peace and clarity descends that is hard to describe.

Keeping hold of that feeling can be a challenge. Those who regularly meditate will know what I am talking about. A daily routine is important, and when I allocate the time to it, I reap the positive benefits.

Your mind needs rest as much as your body

I know when my mind is getting tired and needs to be refreshed. You may be familiar with the feeling of trying to go to bed when you haven't quite managed to turn down the noise in your head. It is as if you are still at work. The mind fails to realise the difference between a real and imagined event; it responds in the same way as if you were still at your desk.

Taking time to meditate before you go to bed, or when you wake up, can have a profound impact on your mental and emotional well-being.

It has required some discipline for me to learn to meditate and to give myself time to practice. I am still work in progress. I do look forward to those little pockets of space that I create for myself. It is always possible to have a special place in your mind that you can take yourself off to in order to relax.

Meditation gives you a sense of being connected rather than being distracted from yourself.

Re-training your brain

I can remember back to when I worked in a Corporate Training manager's role – we used to handwrite our training notes and hand them to our secretary to type them up. I could only plan my training properly if I had written my notes by hand, as that was what I was used to. When I first started using a PC, I couldn't think in the same way. Now, I notice that many people find it hard to write anything at all because they are so used to typing or, even worse, just using their thumbs to swipe a screen!

I also notice that I now often cannot write quick enough to keep up with my thoughts, and that, when I try to do so, my handwriting is a mess. Ideas come to me so quickly that I sometimes find it hard to capture them all at once. When I feel like this I realise that I need to do something to calm myself down and enable me to get the best out of my mind. It is as if nowadays, with the advent of technology, the pace at which our bodies are expected to move is too fast for our Souls to keep up.

This makes complete sense to me. If I just stop and take a moment of quiet time to meditate, I can reset myself. However, if I don't do this and stay in 6th gear, eventually I become muddled and stressed.

You never know the benefits of something if you don't try it out first.

The gains of SLOW

What happens when you go slower? Once you allow yourself the time and space to take a pause, to refresh your mind and to allow your Soul to breathe, wonderful things will start to happen.

You will find yourself enjoying a new sense of clarity, your energy will return, and you will find yourself with a new sense of purpose. Your decision-making will improve, you will know why you are doing what you are doing. It will all make sense.

Taking time out to think is as vital in your life as a good night's sleep. Everything is better when you can face the day with fresh eyes and a light spirit.

Reflections from the *Voice of Slow*

During this section allow your *Voice of Slow* to come forward

The *Voice of Slow* wants the best for you. It knows you are enough, just as you are. Listen to this gentle voice and trust in its intentions.

So, what can you do to go slower?

The first thing is to recognise that you need to take time out to think. Time to do nothing, time to relax.

Learning to meditate will help you to gain control of your butterfly mind and harness the natural energy of your Soul.

Take yourself out of your normal day-to-day routine and do something different. Give your brain a holiday, a rest from what it normally thinks about.

Practice going a bit slower. Slow down the number of things that you pack into a day. Stop talking as much. Listen more.

Give yourself some silent time every day.

What can you let go of that is no longer serving you in your life or business?

What is weighing you down?

Where could you go slower and be more effective?

Giving yourself permission to go slower, to let go of those things that are no longer serving you and give yourself some time is important. You will not only feel better but will accomplish so much more of what is important to you.

7. Letting go to stress less

"Knowledge is learning some-thing every day, wisdom is let-ting go of something every day"

Zen proverb

This chapter is about recognising that **we are responsible for creating much of the stress** we have in our lives. Hence, we also have the power to reduce this stress, by learning to let go.

You must first understand how you create your own stresses; this will enable you to gain control over your thoughts and emotions. Only then, will you be able to let go of the things that stress you.

Ask yourself

- How much of the stress in our lives is caused by what we do to ourselves?

- How much stress is caused by what we hold onto, in our heads or our hearts?

Stress Less

The words we use when we talk to ourselves can either cause us stress or calm us down – it is all a matter of focus.

Our bodies respond in the same way to what we perceive to be a threat as it does to what actually is dangerous. (This stress response is described in Chapter One)

Think back to the last time you were nervous about doing something What were your thoughts and how did they impact on your body?

I can remember when I was about to deliver my first five-minute talk on *The Voice of Slow* at the *Professional Speaking Association (PSA)* meeting. It was the start of my journey to deliver these powerful messages, and I desperately wanted to be able to get them out in the right way for people. I didn't want to let *The Voice of Slow* down.

It is incredibly hard to get a powerful message across in just five minutes! So, I was afraid of going over my time limit, I was scared about speaking for the first time in front of my peers, and I was worried about they might think of me? It was critical for me to get everything spot on.

Pay attention to the language I am using now to describe how I was feeling back then. You can see the state I was getting myself into; I was nervous but excited . . . I was creating stress in myself.

If I had not known how to change my state of mind, I may well have messed up. I started thinking about how I wanted the speech to go, as opposed to what might happen if I forgot my words. I thought about what I wanted the audience to think, feel, and do having listened to my five minutes from *The Voice of Slow*. I projected outwards, and let go of my inwardly-focused fears.

The presentation went very well.

In Chapter Four, I explained how your internal dialogue (i.e. what you say to yourself) and how you use your imagination can create a feeling inside you, a state of mind, which can be either useful or detrimental.

Being aware of how you influence your own stress levels will free you up to make different choices.

Talking about stressful things creates more stress

Remember back to a time when you have had a bad day at work, or at home, and started telling your partner about it in the evening. What happened to you when you did that?

The more you talk about something stressful, the more you end up reliving it, and the more agitated you become. Yes, it is good to get things off your chest, but be aware of what can happen when you keep going over the same thing, again and again. Letting go of talking about stressful things helps to create the space to start dealing with whatever is causing that stress in the first place. It's the first step.

When the past becomes the present

Be aware of how you create your own stress by referencing painful situations from your past.

I know that, over the years, I have always found it hard to let go at the end of my relationships. I would say it used to take me at least two to three years to get over any breakup, even if it was my decision at the time. I would repeatedly go over what went wrong, give myself a hard time, and hold onto thoughts of reconciliation. Then, once I realised that there could be no going back, I would start to worry that I could never feel the same way about anybody else. I would talk endlessly to my girlfriends about each painful break-up, no doubt driving them all to distraction in the process!

Giving time away

I now realise how much of my life I gave to these men, not just when I was with them, but in all the years I spent talking about them and thinking about what might have been if only this, or that, had happened. I could have spent this time concentrating upon healing myself rather than re-enforcing all the pain I had suffered. And, at the end of the day, what difference did my inability to let go really make?

I remember one relationship which ended particularly painfully. During the time I spent going over and over it, trying to understand what happened, he had let go, moved on, married, and had had children.

We often don't realise what we are doing to ourselves unless somebody gently makes us aware of it. I would love some of that time back, but sadly, it has gone forever.

I know now that my inability to let go in relationships was connected to my past, having grown up with parents who were not happy together. I remember always being worried about them breaking up and keeping myself happy by telling myself that it wasn't going to happen. However, when it eventually did happen, my sister and I lost contact for many years with our father, whom we loved very much. I felt like I had experienced a break-up myself, at first-hand. Both our parents moved on in their own different ways, leaving us to grieve the loss of our family and our childhood. It would be many years before I could fully let go of the anger and the sadness.

Take the learning and let go

The ability to learn from painful situations and to know when to let go of them is something that we can all teach ourselves to do. There is always a choice. There is almost always something you need to learn first before you can let it go.

The real strength is knowing when it is time to let go of the pain to be able to move forward, to cut the cord and let it float away.

Letting go of worry

We all worry about things from time to time; it is normal. But what exactly is *'worry'* and how does it affect us?

Worry occurs when you keep thinking about the potential negative outcomes of a situation. When you worry, you must listen to negative, stressful words inside your head, and consequently, you experience the same pain, even though the situation you are worried about hasn't actually happened yet!

Have you ever said to yourself, *'I wish I hadn't spent so much time worrying about that?'* when the eventual outcome turned out to be better than you had expected? It may have been an exam you were taking, a job interview, or some other situation which meant a great deal to you.

We often worry when something really matters to us and, deep down, we want it all to be OK. The challenge is that worry causes you stress and stress rarely aids a positive outcome. Some people say they need to worry to get themselves moving and motivated, to prevent the potential negative outcome that they have already created in their heads. If you are not aware of what you are doing to yourself, this may happen automatically.

The next time you catch yourself worrying, be aware of:

- What you are saying to yourself
- The words are you using
- The negative images you have created in your mind
- Ask yourself if they are helping you (probably not!)

Can we control our own reaction to worry?

We all have our own secret worries, ones which we do not tell other people, but which are present all the same. I have worried about lots of things over the years – some of these worries were well-founded, others I could probably have lived without.

A recurrent worry for me has always been worrying about running out of work, not having enough money, or spending too much time on things that don't work out.

Of course, like many independent business owners, I have worked on things that haven't sold as well as I would have liked, I have had jobs that didn't turn out as planned, and I have had periods of feast and famine work-wise. However, when I think about it, I have also had things that have worked out well and that have been in demand – I haven't really lacked anything at all.

If I had managed to stop all that unnecessary worrying, and instead, been able to focus on what was working for me, I might have felt differently.

Switching the focus

Worry can often be our imaginations playing cruel games with us, our egos turning up to shake us up a bit and distract us from the feelings of peace and joy that we could access, if only we could hear our *Voice of Slow*.

Our true power comes from being able to switch the focus. To catch yourself worrying and challenge your own thinking. To ask yourself calmly whether the thoughts you are creating in your mind are real or imagined? Are they helping or hindering the situation? Is there another way of looking at the same issue?

Your thoughts can either give you energy or take it away. You can become the master of your thoughts and your worries, as soon as you allow yourself time and space to become consciously aware of what is happening. You can choose to let go of worry and you can turn it into a more positive emotion.

For example, you might be worried about an important exam and the worry motivates you to study for it. However, you proceed to work yourself up with worry because this is an exam and there could be consequences if you don't pass. This is the point at which you can change your thought process.

Think about how good it will feel when you find out that you can answer the questions because you are well-prepared. Think about how much passing this exam matters and what it will help you to achieve. Imagine a great result. These thoughts will create a surge of energy in your body and mind – they will help you, just as the worries would have hindered you.

Almost daily, I catch myself slipping into *'worry mode'*. However, I am now able to catch myself quickly, and once I do, I am in a position to tell myself to think differently and to look at things from another angle.

So, notice what it is that you are worrying about and ask yourself whether you could look at it from a different viewpoint, from a place where things could turn out well, where your worries could prove unfounded. It won't always turn out how you imagined, but at least you have now created a situation where a positive outcome is possible.

Letting go of anger

Anger is an emotion that causes stress when expressed both internally for ourselves, and externally for others.

Anger is generated when something is *'not right'*, according to our view of the world. Whilst we may be completely justified in expressing our feelings of anger, how we deal with it will affect our emotional state.

Feelings of anger can live with us for years. When you relive a past experience, if the feelings of anger are still present, you will feel it in your body, hear it in the tone of your voice, and be able to experience the same emotions.

A few years ago, an old friend from the past reconnected with me and came over for an evening. The last time I had last seen her, almost eight years previously, she had been having problems obtaining a full-time commitment from the man she loved. However, as far as I was aware, she was now happily living with this man. When we met up, I had expected a nice relaxed evening, catching up over a glass of wine. It didn't quite turn out that way. Asking her about her partner triggered off an entire evening of screaming and shouting about everything from his kids, his attitude, the amount of time they spent together, the fact that they weren't married, her lack of trust in him, and much more besides. Try as I might to get her to look at the good, she just couldn't. As far as I could see, the situation was a lot better than it had been eight years previously, but she was still living with her past anger. She had not been able to let go. She was still living with the legacy of the past as if it was the present.

I eventually managed to calm her down and helped her to explore what was working well between them, asking her what she ideally wanted to improve. This enabled her mind to move in a different direction, away from the anger, and towards a place of possibility. There were still many painful issues, that could not be all resolved with a simple chat, but at least by having the space to express how she was feeling, she realised that it was the anger that she was carrying which was holding back their chances of happiness. She had to first let it out and let it go, to be able to move on.

The thing with anger is that it can rise up from nowhere unexpectedly. It can be triggered off by something minor, but usually, the source of the pain we are expressing comes from a much deeper place. Some people have to express their anger openly, whilst others are able to deal with it more calmly within themselves.

The *Voice of Slow* would deal with anger calmly. It would ask what the anger was really about, as often it is not the situation itself.

I have lived with angry people in the past. My mother used to fly off the handle at minor things, to make an issue out of something which I didn't see as a problem. She was like a smouldering volcano, which you never quite knew when was going to erupt. I was very wary of this and quickly formed the opinion that you should not express your anger in a way which upsets other people. Consequently, I have always tried to keep my anger in check.

My mother's anger was actually connected with her unhappy relationship with my father, by whom she felt unloved. It was also connected to her past, having been criticised by her older sister for most of her childhood. So, she lacked confidence, and although her anger erupted over little things, they were really related to something much larger below the surface. Now that I am older and wiser, I can understand that. She is a much more peaceful person now, having lived on her own for many years. She is happy with what she has and who she is. She has let go of a lot of the anger and resentment she felt as a younger woman.

I have always disliked people who express anger in what I would describe as an *'inappropriate'* way. However, somehow these were the very people I tended to attract into my own life! The person I married when I was 28 years old (a marriage which lasted only a year I hasten to add!) turned into somebody who constantly criticised me, becoming moody over even the smallest things. Likewise, later in life, I spent over four years with a man who had even worse anger issues. I eventually had the courage to exit that relationship, despite still having feelings for him. Spending my life with somebody who could not let go of their anger was not where I wanted for be.

How you let go of anger

We can all get angry about things; it is how you deal with them that matters. Learning to step back and let go of the need to express anger, demonstrates maturity and wisdom.

Your *Voice of Slow* would always question what gave rise to this anger in order to help you move forwards with kindness and peace.

When dealing with others who are angry, I have learnt to listen. To not let it affect me. To put up a protective shield to enable me to step outside of the emotions I experience in order to try to understand what is behind their anger. In this way, I am able to observe rather than being drawn into the situation. I am now more able to deal calmly with people who express their anger inappropriately. I can stand my ground and tell them when their communication is not acceptable. I may be shaking inside when I do so – but at least I can do it.

The result of this shift in attitude has been a change in the amount of *'angry'* people whom I attract into my life. Maybe one of the life lessons for me has been about learning to deal with it.

Let it go

So, if you relate to this, knowing that you have anger which you need to deal with, or emotions from the past which you need to let go of, this may be the time to listen to your own *Voice of Slow*. The voice that wants you to be happy and peaceful.

When you are about to get angry about something, ask yourself how big a deal it really is. Take a deep breath and just let it go. See it fly away high in the sky like a balloon when you let go of the string.

Forgive and let go

Being able to forgive is a powerful way of letting go of any negative emotions we hold on to. When something bad happens to us that hurts us deeply, it can be incredibly hard to let go of the feelings of anger, resentment, upset that go with the pain we are suffering. The problem is that, unless we do let go and forgive, it is us that end up suffering the most.

Hard though it may be, forgiveness can set you free.

Sorry can be the hardest word to say

If you have messed up (as we all do from time to time), or if something is your fault and has caused somebody else pain or difficulty, then saying sorry is important. For some people, it can be impossible. Many of my girlfriends have complained over the years of their partners always having to have the last word, of needing to be right whatever the disagreement.

I can remember being in the same situation myself, with one of my 'angry relationship partners'. He was never wrong. He never said sorry. I used to think I had broad shoulders and could forgive. I did this to make it easier for myself. I didn't want to carry the burden of the disagreement. It was my way of closing the door on it, of letting it go. I wished he had been able to say sorry, since it would have made everything so much easier to deal with.

Can you say sorry? Are you able to let go of being right?

Holding onto grudges and resentments will only make you feel bad and unhappy in the long run, so why hold on?

There are small things which can be let go off more easily and there are bigger, more painful matters, which will involve a longer process.

These are complex areas but the simple facts are that what you hold on to is what you feel. If you can forgive or say sorry, there will be a release which will be positive for you.

Your *Voice of Slow* wants you to be able to forgive when someone or something has hurt you and to say sorry when you recognise that you have behaved in a way that has been difficult or hurtful for others.

Letting go can be one of the hardest things we ever have to do, but at the same time, it can give us the most freedom in our lives.

Reflections from the *Voice of Slow*

During this section allow your *Voice of Slow* to come forward

The *Voice of Slow* wants the best for you. It knows you are enough, just as you are. Listen to this gentle voice and trust in its intentions.

Letting go will probably not be an easy thing to do, and you may need time and understanding. Be gentle on yourself and take your time whilst answering the following questions.

Ask yourself:

What is weighing you down in your life?

What could you let go of to enable you to travel lighter?

What difference could letting go have on your life?

What negative emotions could you let go of? (anger, resentment, guilt)

How could forgiveness free you up?

What could be the first small step you could take?

As you let go you will feel the lightness in your life.

It will get easier as you take the steps.

As your load gets lighter you will be more able to enjoy the present moments of your life.

8. Present is NOW

"Forever is composed of Nows"

Emily Dickinson

This chapter is about becoming aware of the power of **being in the present moment.**

Whilst being able to be in the NOW is one of the true gifts of SLOW, it is a state of being that many find hard. Living in the present moment slows life down and enables inner peace and joy. Everyone can achieve this once they become self-aware.

Ask yourself

- Are you aware of the present moments in your life?

- Are you aware of being present?

- Are you aware of just being still?

Living in the moment

We can only ever really live in the *present moment* as that is all there ever is for any of us. Many people find it hard to be where they are at any given moment, fully present, feeling, seeing and hearing what is happening in the *'now'*, whilst giving something or somebody their full, undivided attention.

Most the time we are somewhere else; distracted by a message on our phones when sitting in a café with friends, thinking about what we are going to do that evening whilst sitting in an important work meeting, thinking about the tasks we should be doing when we take a break to go for a walk.

The gift

Being present can be very relaxing because your mind only needs to deal with one thing – the present. That is why it is often called a gift. Eckhart Tolle author of *The Power of Now* writes about the rewarding journey we can all make back to the peace and stillness that is available to us, simply by surrendering to the present moment.

What is being present like?

We've all had those fleeting experiences of being completely present in our lives and have experienced how peaceful and relaxing that can be.

A business colleague of mine recently told me how much better he felt when he took three days out of his busy schedule to go sailing on a barge down the Thames. The slowness of the boat's movement, the beautiful river views, and the simplicity of the days watching kingfishers feeding from the banks lulled him into a state of being that he had not experienced for a long time. He was able to take the breath he needed and let go fully. He wasn't distracted by the pressure to do something, to take action, or to have a plan. He could just be at one with nature and with himself.

Being present can also be quite simply when you are fully absorbed in something you love doing. It could be gardening, painting, making music, playing with your kids, running, anything that gets you into a state of just being there fully in the moment. It is why you feel so good when you spend some time doing these things; you are fully absorbed in the present and nothing else exists.

One of the reasons I like long-distance running (not that I am much good at it, I should quickly add!) is that once I hit about eight miles and get into a rhythm, I feel a lift, a sense of being in a sort of flow state. All I seem to notice is what is happening at that moment; all other thoughts drift away. If you are a runner you may know what I am talking about?

The thing about being present is that it is real! It is the only place we can be, yet, because so much of our life is lived through our minds and our thoughts, we are, for the most part, disconnected.

The faster we think the faster we go

Technology makes our lives so much faster. Some may say this is better for us. But is it really? Does it actually distract us from the present moment?

The other day, I was having a conversation with somebody about our student life, and we were discussing how learning is so much different now compared to when we were students. Nowadays you can find the answer to pretty much anything with a quick Google search. Compare this to the time we used to spend reading or researching books in a library . . . positively pedestrian by today's standards!

I can still remember the feeling of spending time in the silence of a library researching for an essay. It was peaceful. Taking your time to find the answer was OK. Our essays were handwritten and there was something nice about that. You had time to think, to reflect, without the feeling of skimming over things and of only needing to take in the overview.

I don't remember the feeling of information overload that I often feel today.

The way life is now can make it harder to be mindful and present. There is always so much to offload before you have the space to hear your own voice.

Slowing down and really paying attention to things is almost like asking an unused muscle to lift a heavy weight. It is tough and hard work. The inclination is always to move on quickly.

Mindfulness matters

When you slow down and savour moments in your life, the pleasure you receive will be enhanced.

Just like eating chocolate. If you grab a bar and eat it quickly, the pleasure will be short-lived, and you probably just want another bar immediately. However, if you take just one piece and really savour it, allowing yourself to enjoy the taste and the texture, you will gain far more in terms of real pleasure.

Speed can distract from pleasure

When you take a bus the journey usually takes longer, but you have time to people watch and to pay more attention to the places you pass by. Which is relaxing.

When you walk, instead of jump in the car, you feel each step, and your connection to the journey is stronger.

If you pay attention to what you see and hear, the pleasure you gain will be enhanced. Try it next time you go for a walk. Listen to the birds singing, look closely at the flowers, trees, feel the breeze brushing against your skin. That is 'present moment living'.

Slowing your mind down enables you to be more aware. More aware of the simple pleasurable things in your life, the things you may miss or become blind to when your thoughts are constantly switching between the past or the future.

Missing moments in your life by not being present

All our lives are simply a series of *'present'* moments.

If you live your life always wanting to be somewhere else, then you risk missing out on what is important in the here and now. It is so tempting to set a future goal and then to focus upon what it will be like when you have achieved it. By doing that though, you are living in the future and not in the present.

At present, I am aware of how much I enjoy writing this book and how peaceful I feel during the process. It is as if everything else drops away and all I can hear are the words I want to set down on paper. My thoughts seem to jump out of my mind into each chapter.

I have a long-standing company client who, in the years of working with me, more than doubled their turnover and profits. Recently, the owners decided they wanted to increase turnover by half a million and raised their targets accordingly. Having just enjoyed their best-ever summer for sales, instead of celebrating and enjoying this achievement, they found themselves focusing on the fact that they were still behind on their new targets. They were seeing *'lack'* as opposed to *'abundance'*. So, we had a conversation about how to be *'present'* and the need to celebrate the *'now'* as well as having an eye on future targets. They reported that soon after, they felt the stress melt away, simply by appreciating what they had already achieved.

Random thoughts can take you away from your present

In the last chapter, I wrote about worry. As soon as we start worrying, our ability to stay present disappears. Our minds starting to behave like a young child darting around in lots of different directions.

Are you aware of when you are not being present? For example, when going on holiday and thinking about work for most of the time. Or (in my case) attending a meditation class and using the time to plan your week.

Being present is when you are immersed in the moment, living and feeling it, surrendering to that moment.

The courage to be present

I have talked about my own time spent walking the Camino de Santiago over the last few years; every time I go, it reminds me how wonderful it is to live in the moment.

I must take myself out of my normal life to do it. I can remember at the beginning of these trips, constantly thinking about my life and my work. I had created the time and space but my mind was still crowded. However, after a while, the simple routine and exhaustion of walking 30km per day enabled me to experience what it is like to turn off that noise in your head and just be 'present' with each day.

It can be scary to unplug completely, especially for somebody like me whose instinct is to hold on to everything, just in case I lose it completely!

Letting go of all the chatter in my head wasn't easy – I was aware of how much I could miss by allowing worry to slip back in when it wasn't wanted. Worries about not being able to get back on track when I returned to work, worries about what if I was missing out by taking so much time off . . .you name it, I could worry about it!

However, the simple daily process of *'Walk – Eat – Sleep – Repeat'* eventually became an extended meditation. Moving like we were born to do every day, with only simplest things to think about, forces you to relax and allow yourself just to be with the moment.

The simplicity of what you are doing every day changes your perspective. A hot coffee in the morning after walking 5km tastes so good. A warm comfortable bed at night. You notice the flowers, the trees, and connect with the energy of all the nature around you. Being present can give you huge surges of pleasure!

Bringing the present back

The daily practice of being present is so important. Think of it like building a muscle. If you practice it daily, even for just a short time, it will have an impact and eventually, you will gain more control over those random thoughts. I have been conscious of this for some time now and allow my *Voice of Slow* to remind me of the importance of being present every day.

Switching it all off

We all need some quiet time.

Our minds are bombarded with information every day. From the minute we get up to the minute we close our eyes to go to sleep, there is always something that could be on your mind if you let it.

At the end of a busy day, my mind can feel like it has really been put through its paces, stretched to the limit, needing a break. It needs to be empty of all thoughts, clear of all thinking, free of all the day's information. It needs some quiet time, to be blank and not disturbed.

So, every day I give my mind some space.

I practice one of these simple routines.

I go up to a quiet room on top floor of my house, put on one of my meditation CDs, shut the door, light a candle and give myself 30 minutes of mind-clearing time.

Or I go for a walk along the river near my home and stop for 10 minutes to listen to the silence.

Or I just sit in silence, alone for twenty minutes doing absolutely nothing, letting any thoughts I have just drift away up into the clouds.

I find these simple techniques all help me to quieten my mind down. As a result, I feel fresher and more alert. If I allow myself to be too busy and miss a few days, I really do notice the difference, as the feeling of overload increases and it becomes increasingly harder to make clear decisions.

Do you recognise this in yourself?

Reflections from the *Voice of Slow*

During this section allow your Voice of Slow to come forward.

The *Voice of Slow* wants the best for you. It knows you are enough, just as you are. Listen to this gentle voice and trust in its intentions.

Experience the impact of being present

Your mind deserves to be kept healthy and fresh. It is one of your most valuable assets.

What could you do for your mind to give it the rest it needs?

Start by giving yourself five minutes a day just to sit still. Close your eyes and focus on your breathing. Let your shoulders drop. Picture a blue sky with clouds and every time a thought comes in . . . just imagine it drifting away.

As time goes by, you may be able to extend this time.

The main thing is just to do it. It doesn't have to be perfect

---

Reflections

When do you notice that you are *'present'*?

When are you not *'present'*? What distractions are you aware of?

What could you do to spend more time, relishing the present moment?

The real gift the *'present'* has for you is to show you that what you already have inside can provide you with all the happiness you desire. When you are fully present, you will gain access to more personal peace and joy.

Enjoy the moments of your life, as these moments are all we ever really have.

9. Trust

"Our way is not soft grass, it's a mountain path with lots of rocks, but it goes upwards, forward towards the sun"

Ruth Westheimer

This chapter is all about **trust** – how important it is to have trust in ourselves and on our path in life. It is also about understanding how issues of trust can affect you and how to become more aware of the important signs in your life.

Trust is like a tree with deep roots; solid and reliable. Trust can be shaken in a storm but if its roots are strong enough, it will hold firm.

Trusting yourself and your journey can be the hardest lesson. Our biggest challenge is often to ourselves.

Ask yourself

- Is trust an issue for you?
- Are you aware of the signs in your life that light your way?

Trust

Trust is a big word. As I say it, I take a deep breath. It is what it is all about. Trust in yourself and trust that your journey is the right one for you.

At a deeper level, I believe that we are all here to learn the lessons we need most. The path that we must travel contains obstacles which block our way and the turnings we take on that path are present for good reasons. These lessons may not always be immediately obvious but, upon reflection, there are always connections with the links in the chain that make up our lives.

Think about your own journey for a moment and the word 'trust'. What does that word mean to you? What immediately springs to mind?

Have you always trusted that the route you are on through life is the right one for you?

You are where you are

It may not have been a perfectly straight road. If it had been, with no setbacks or obstacles, what opportunities would there be for learnings?

Remember the earlier quote, *'The Ox would not know it was strong unless it had to pull a cart'*? In other words, we would not be where we are today if it were not for all our struggles and strife. It is through these struggles that we grow, as we learn and become stronger on the inside. When things go wrong and we face painful times, it can be hard to maintain that vital trust in the bigger picture.

Your island is not the only world

In life, we all build our own *'islands'*; the paths we construct, and the flowers or shrubs we plant, all represent our own mental make-up, whilst our experiences inform our perception of life. Our islands represent our own personal worlds. On the surface, these islands may seem different, but underneath they are all connected to the same sea. Imagine a vast expanse which links all these islands together. We are all the same at a deeper level – it is only on the surface that we appear different.

Our journeys in life begin from the same destination and will eventually return us to the same place. It is what is in-between that is unique for all of us.

The law of repetition

I have always been a believer in the Law of Repetition (I don't know if this is what it is called, but if it wasn't, it is now!) by which I mean, if we fail to learn the lessons we are here to learn, they will keep coming back to us in different ways until we take them on board. We can't cheat our own life plans. We can't hide our lack of trust and pretend that we are learning when we are not.

I know that to be true of my life. When I look back, I can see patterns, things that seem to happen over and over until I finally learn the lessons I need to learn, and only then do I experience a shift, a change in my perceptions. I am now aware of this happening in a way that I was not when I was younger.

Have you noticed this kind of pattern in your life?

Trust issues

I know one of my big issues has been trust. Trust in myself, my abilities, my gifts, and trust in financial abundance to enable me to live freely and share my gifts. I have had other issues too, trust in long-term love is one of them. I have always wanted it, craved it almost, but in a funny way it has always been elusive, there has always been a reason why I have not been able to enjoy a long-term one-to-one committed relationship, despite it being something I have always wanted to have. I have had good long relationships but never been able to fully relax and be in a situation where I was completely free to be with the person I love. As I write this book I am in a loving relationship, but it still has its blocks (for various reasons outside of my personal control) to a full secure commitment. These are my lessons with challenges to learn from which I am very much aware of. I know one of my lessons has been in learning to love and trust myself which I have needed to access, to survive some of the losses I have had to face.

I have also found the journey to trust in financial abundance a challenge, despite always actually having had enough. I have lived with ups and downs of feast and famine which is typical of people working in the coaching and training business, yet I have managed to survive well enough for over 20 years. I have always been scared, and if you scratched below the surface you would most certainly find wobbly founda-tions, but I know that learning to trust in this and having the courage to follow my heart more than my head is part of this journey. I am doing it now by taking the time to write this book.

If you think about your Island, the routes you have travelled and the buildings you have built brick by brick where are your foundations most shaky? Where does that little voice of fear pipe up and shake your trust? It is there for most of us somewhere . . .

Trust yourself

Learning to trust in ourselves and who we really are is one of our biggest lessons.

We can all be distracted and lured off track by our egos. That little person on your shoulder who wants you to believe that you are defined by your mind, that your material goods rep-resent your worth, and that what you look like on the out-side is who you are on the inside. The truth is that you are not your thoughts. Your thoughts are only thoughts – they are not you. You are much more than this. But you may be asking, 'Who am I really?' What can I trust in?' These are big questions, that many people have spent lifetimes search-ing for the answers to, both inside and outside of them-selves.

Being on a spiritual path myself, I too have been searching. I have had brief moments in my life when I have connected with the power of (what I perceive to be) universal energy. This has happened to me during deep meditations and in a number moments whilst walking the Camino when I heard the *Voice of Slow*. It felt like I was like rising higher, towards a huge space that seemed infinite; I felt lifted, an out of body experience. It only ever lasted for the briefest of moments and then I was back down, but I have sampled enough to feel the gateway of trust opening. Trust in something bigger and greater than just me. Maybe you too have experienced this?

Slow down and trust

I still struggle though. The road to complete trust in myself and the journey I am on is probably the work of many lifetimes.

Patterns repeat until you learn

My work life has been a challenging path, with many mountains to climb. My love life has also presented many hard and painful losses.

I know now that this has all been part of my journey, repeating the same lesson of self-love and trust in different ways until I learn what I need to learn.

As you read these words you may be thinking of what it is in your life that keeps repeating. Do you see patterns? Have self-love and trust been lessons for you?

We always have choices

It is not always easy. Trust is such a big word and so many things in life come along to rock our boats, that smooth sailing is rarely a possibility. You do always have a choice though. You can choose to focus on 'lack' or you can choose to focus on what you do have. Having an awareness of what is happening to you will light the path for change.

It is necessary to trust in yourself enough to go slower for a while if you need to, to let go of the things that may not be serving you, to give yourself permission to make changes and try something new. At times, it is easy to lose the faith; faith in ourselves and faith that something greater is always possible.

Trusting in the way

Over the years when I took time out to walk many hundreds of miles on various routes of the Camino de Santiago, there were always signs to follow. These signs were either a yellow arrow point in the direction of travel, or the shape of a shell, with the ridges of the shell representing the various routes that all converge upon the same destination, the cathedral in Santiago where Saint James was buried. Saints and pilgrims have walked these routes for centuries following these signs. It was interesting that when I walked this path myself, there were times when the signs were not obvious. You could get lost, especially walking early in the morning when it was only just getting light. You just had to trust that there would be a sign to guide you, and if you went off track, you would somehow be led back. It struck me how many times this happened. I think it was a good lesson in trust and one to bring back to normal life.

When the wrong way is the right way

There are many times in our lives when we feel like we may be on the wrong path, that the route we are taking is going off-track and away from where we think we should be heading.

Maybe it feels wrong but could it still be right? The wrong way can sometimes be the right way.

Think about where you are in your life right now and the paths which have led you to this point. You will have had to face many crossroads where you had to make a decision and choose a path. Had you not taken that path, you might not be sitting here now reading this book?

I can remember listening to my half-sister Marieke when she was only 13, talking about her possible choices. She talked about the different routes she could take in her life and how her choices would influence the person she would marry and the life she would have. She used to find making decisions difficult, worrying about where each different decision would lead. As it turned out, after what she would describe as a wrong turn with her first University choice in Germany, her next choice led her to Liverpool and the UK. After graduating her work experience then took her back to Germany to Berlin where she met and fell in love with a Frenchman. They had a son together which prompted a decision to move to his home town in France.

Now we could not have predicted this when we were walking along the riverside almost 19 years ago. Did Marieke find herself with important decisions to make? Yes, she did. Did she always know what would happen as a result? No, she didn't. However, with some faith and a degree of trust, she took steps which have led her to a happy life with her French husband and son.

The signs are always there when you SLOW down

What are the signs which let you know that something, or someone, or a situation is right for YOU?

If you are racing through life at a great speed, always busy, always multi-tasking, never taking a moment to pause and catch breath, the chances are you could miss the signs in your life which would let you know that something is right (or wrong) for you.

You may not have given yourself time to think about what you really want, so you may not recognise it when it does come along, instead of grasping at something which is not quite right. I am sure everyone has experienced this at some point in their time.

You must know wrong to know right

You must know what is not right, in order to know what is right. So, for every wrong turn, there is a sign for the right one if you pay attention.

It is like walking in the forest with a map – you take the wrong turning and get a bit lost, but you can backtrack, look at the map, take another route, and find the one you were supposed to be on. You learnt which was **not** the way to your destination, and by doing so, discovered the right route.

Trusting your intuition

I have been in many situations, invested time in many projects, spent time with people, or partners, or relationships, when I knew that something wasn't quite right, but continued anyway, hoping everything would work itself out. I didn't quite trust enough in myself and my own intuition.

Often, the signs were there to enable me to learn and move on, but the more I ignored them, the worse they became. It was as if the signs had to scream at me to get me to listen, presenting me with more pain until I eventually shifted and moved, taking the learning with me.

I have also experienced the opposite when the situation, personal relationship, project, or partnership just flowed. It was easy, smooth, and fun – things worked out, and went from strength to strength. When I think back to these situations, the signs were there too; signs to appreciate what I had and how to learn from it, signs to commit to memory so they could be recognised when they appeared again in the future.

So, to answer the question – what are the signs that let you know if something is right for you? I think you probably know most of the answers already.

Here are some of the indicators:

- There was a coincidence or indicator early on
- It *'felt'* right not wrong
- It flowed as opposed to being continually blocked
- It was easy as opposed to being continually difficult
- It gave you pleasure rather than pain
- You enjoyed the journey as opposed to hating the process
- You could be yourself as opposed to feeling false

Signs on your journey through life are everywhere when you slow down and allow yourself time and space to see them.

Get out of your own way and trust

We can all get in our own way at times.

We overthink things and worry too much, losing trust in ourselves and our path. This happens to everyone, no matter how outwardly successful they appear on the surface.

Ego will try it on with self-sabotaging words, reminding us of our weaknesses, talking us out of the things that should give us joy, telling us that what we can't do. The trick is not to listen.

Reflections from the *Voice of Slow*

During this section allow your *Voice of Slow* to come forward

The *Voice of Slow* wants the best for you. It knows you are enough, just as you are. Listen to this gentle voice and trust in its intentions.

Reflections:

What difficult or challenging situations have you noticed repeating in your life?

Have there been recurring themes?

What lessons are you aware of?

What are you aware of that you lack trust in?

What caused that?

What do you trust?

What would you most like to trust in? Say it out loud, *"I trust in . . ."*, and frame it in positive words.

Notice how this feels and repeat it as often and you can.

You will see and feel a shift. Trust is a powerful force. The most important person you can trust in is yourself. Trust in your inner spirit that always has the best intentions, that knows the right way even when things are tough.

Trust in yourself first and everything else will fall into place.

10. The Power of Gratitude and Kindness

"Gratitude is heaven itself"

William Blake

This chapter is about two words – **gratitude and kindness;** two words which give so much, but which are so often neglected.

Everybody can experience greater happiness when they pay attention to the right things. Giving and receiving kindness in your life will increase your feelings of happiness – it will allow you to focus on what you have got as opposed to what you lack.

Ask yourself

- Are you aware of the power of gratitude?

- Do you value kindness?

The Power of Gratitude and Kindness

Think about the last time someone did something really kind for you? It might not have been a grand gesture; maybe it was something simple, yet it showed you that another person cared. Maybe it was from somebody you knew well, or maybe it was an act of kindness from a complete stranger?

As we rush through life, it is easy to miss these small gestures that are made every day. When noticed, and appreciated, these simple acts of kindness provide a huge boost.

Slowing down gives you a chance to be more aware of the power of kindness, both in yourself and in others.

Value kindness

Kindness is a quality I value very highly. I notice it in others and take time to try to be kind wherever I can.

I have an extremely kind friend called Jan, who is always putting others first. She does those little things which could go unnoticed if you failed to pay attention. She stocks up her neighbours' fridges when they are returning from holiday, she often pops in unexpectedly when she suspects a friend has been feeling down about something, she picks up little gifts she thinks you might like even when it is not your birthday. She is a foot health practitioner, with many elderly clients, and the number of little extra things she does for them when she visits really make me smile. She posts letters, puts away shopping, walks dogs, fixes TVs and so much more. It is simply in her nature to be kind.

My partner Matt is also kind. He once filled a tiny hole in a door of mine that was letting in cold air. It was so small it could have gone unnoticed. He didn't tell me what he had done, but I saw it and I appreciated it. No one had ever filled a hole in a door for me! It was a small thing but actually, it represented something much bigger. I was with a kind man and that was very important to me. I have always noticed and appreciated the little things he does and as a result, this has made our relationship stronger.

Things that get in the way of kindness

Acts of kindness are important, both at work and at home.

At work, the pressure to complete agendas, hit targets, or meet deadlines often means that kindness is forgotten. In tougher corporate environments, kindness can be associated with weakness. Of course, we know that is not necessarily true, but the culture which some organisations create tends not to support day-to-day kindness. Fear can stop people being kind.

Here are some examples:

- If I help this person, I will get involved and then I will be expected to keep doing so.

- If I am kind, somebody will take advantage of me I may not be respected if I show my softer side.

- If I stop what I am doing to help another person, I may not get what I want done.

- No one has ever been kind to me, so why should I bother to be kind to others?

You can understand how, with beliefs like that around, why many people are not as kind as they could be. If you are reading this and any of the above beliefs resonate with you, take this opportunity to ask yourself why this should be?

Are they your beliefs or somebody else's? What could be another way of thinking about it?

Can kindness make me vulnerable?

I know that deep down my mother is kind, but she does suffer from a fear of getting involved and having somebody take advantage of her if she gives too much.

My late grandmother Peggy didn't have a kindness filter. She would have given someone the shirt off her back if she thought it might help them. Being the oldest girl in a poor family of 10 children, she always had to put others before herself. I remember her telling me that when she was given a boiled sweet she used to share it with all nine of her brothers and sisters so they all could have a few sucks!

She always pressed a £10 note into my hand whenever I went to see her, even when she was on a pension and I was working. She used to say it made her feel good, so I had to take it. I could write a whole book about the number of kind gestures that I saw her make in her lifetime. She always took the time to be kind.

Kindness is a choice

Kindness is something you can learn to be. If you were lucky enough to see kindness in your parents, grandparents, or other family members when you were younger and valued it, the likelihood is that you may find it easier to practice the art yourself. Or it could be that you have never experienced much kindness in your life and wished you had, so now you give more to those around you.

As I have written in previous chapters, it is our life story which shapes how we are. Today though, you have a choice. You can choose to be kind. You can choose to be aware of the kindness that you have in your life, no matter how small the gesture is.

It is also as important to be kind to yourself. Giving yourself time, looking after yourself and listening to your *Voice of Slow*.

Notice Acts of Kindness for a day

Just as an experiment, notice how many acts of kindness you see happening in your place of work or at home this week.

Write them down. It doesn't matter how small they are, just pay attention and observe. If they involve you, recognise them with thanks.

Be extra kind for a day

Why not choose to do something kind for somebody in your place of work each day and notice the impact it has on both you and them?

It might be making them a tea or coffee, helping them with a project, giving them an introduction that was important to them, or complementing them on a particular achievement.

Or it might be when at home, giving extra time to listen to a friend, helping someone out, offering a kind word.

When you give a genuine act of kindness from the heart, the positive energy that goes with it is responsible for the lift it gives to both you and the person who chose to be kind.

When you realise how important kindness is in your life, both giving and receiving, it is something you can change and hence have more access to. It is one of those things in life that is free and adds great richness.

Gratitude

In the race towards your goals in life, it can be easy to lose sight of what you have already got that is good.

If you are feeling a lack in your life, if you focus on it, talk about it, think about it, and worry about it, then you will certainly get an empty feeling. If on the other hand, you switch your thoughts to what you have in your life that you are grateful for, you will soon change that empty feeling to one of fulfilment.

It often takes having less to recognise what you have got to be grateful for. When life is lived at a fast pace, it is easy to take everything for granted. You forget to be humble. Remember to recognise how blessed you already are.

Walking the Caminos simplified my life for a while. It also helped me to be more grateful for simple things.

Because walking slows you down, you pay attention in a different way to the natural world around you. You start to really appreciate the simple pleasures. I appreciated every bed I slept in, every meal I ate, every hot coffee I drank. I was very grateful to be able to do it. I was fit and healthy enough to walk the distances every day and be outside in nature. The more I reminded myself of how lucky and grateful I was, the happier I felt. My senses were alive. So much of what we can allow to happen to us in our normal routine can numb our senses. We forget to say a silent 'Thank you' for what we have. If we are not careful, we can race along, taking everything we have for granted.

I have lived long enough and experienced enough pain in my life to know that not recognising what you have got while you have it, is a big mistake. I never waste a day now (well maybe I do, sometimes!) I do things whilst I can. If I forget to be grateful, I either remind myself silently or say it out loud. Even now, when I face pain and hardship, I still attempt to look for the simple things to be grateful for. They are there even in the darkest hour. You can change your state instantly by being grateful, especially during tough times. There is always something there if you are aware.

Reflections from the *Voice of Slow*

During this section allow your *Voice of Slow* to come forward.

The *Voice of Slow* wants the best for you. It knows you are enough, just as you are. Listen to this gentle voice and trust in its intentions.

Kindness and gratitude are powerful forces in our lives. They both are so simple to do yet often forgotten. By bringing more kindness and gratitude into your life you will enhance your feelings of joy and happiness.

Reflections on Kindness

Who is kind to you?

What gestures of kindness have you noticed this week?

What have you done this week that is kind?

How can you add more kindness to your life?

Kindness starts with giving. Giving time can be kind too, so slow down and give yourself time for those random acts of kindness. Be grateful for the kindness you see in your life. Kindness is enriching. Remember to be kind to yourself too.

Reflections on Gratitude

What have you got to be grateful for in your life?

Make a list.

Daily thoughts about what you are grateful for can be very empowering.

Don't wait until something is taken away for you to miss it.

Give it your attention now and say thanks.

You will notice the impact this has on your feeling of happiness and well-being.

11. Listen to your music

"Time gives good advice"

Maltese proverb

This chapter is all about **finding and honouring** our music.

We all have music inside us; we just need to create time and space to hear it. Your music will guide you to what you want to do with your life and to what makes you happy.

Ask yourself

- Do you give yourself time to hear your own music?

- Do you know what makes you happy?

Listen to your music

In our busy lives, communication is a constant background presence. There is so much interaction, so much talking, both online and offline, which can, at times, be overwhelming. There is very little silence. These days if we want silence, we must seek it out.

I am of the age where the internet, social media, and mobile phones have all become an integral part of my life. I didn't grow up with them though – I can still remember life before mobile phones.

It can be hard to switch off in today's culture of continuous communication. Checking your emails anywhere, posting on Facebook, or chatting via WhatsApp can all become addictive. And for the younger generation, this is the norm.

Slowing down, or even switching off, all communication channels would be a horror story for many people. But if we never give ourselves time to press pause on this ever-present stream of communication, how do we know what effect it is having on us? I know it exhausts me at times. I like to talk and I enjoy connecting with people, but I also need of periods of silence to rebalance myself.

Are we all talking too much?

Do you like to talk?

I do and am lucky that my work that involves a lot of interaction. However, if I am not too careful, it can become overly intense. When it comes to the end of the day, I just need to shut down and be silent. I am lucky that I can make time for this in my day. I make sure that I balance periods of intense chat with those of solitude. Just as I love to talk, I also love the sound of silence. In fact, sitting here beside my fire in my kitchen writing these words, I almost feel like I am breathing in silence, it is so beautiful.

My friend mentioned booking a holiday the other day, saying that she really needed to have some down time. Her work involves people and as she is a friendly, warm person who likes to entertain, she can end up talking all day long. She said she had started to feel 'wired up' like she had become like a stuck record playing over and over. She needs some space to hear her own music.

The courage to be silent

It can take courage to be alone and be silent. There can always be an urge to fill the space with noise. To distract ourselves from just being with ourselves. Some people who live alone find this easy other not so. How much silent time do you have in your life?

Once you can access your inner peace, you can be free. Free from the need always to have something going on in your life. You can just be happy with the silence surrounding you.

Slow down your thoughts to listen

To hear your own music, you need to start from a place of silence. When your mind is continually jumping from one thing to the next, it is hard to hear the call of your music.

I can recall busy periods in my life working one-to-one with worried business owners to facilitate their thinking processes, I needed to concentrate to help them through. Some meetings were like mental ping pong; I would come back home barely able to think, let alone talk. At that point in time, I wasn't giving myself time to hear my own music. And I felt it.

It wasn't until I immersed myself in the silence of my Camino walks that I was eventually able to hear myself again. The peace of those mornings as the sun rose to greet the new day was so silent that you could hear your every breath. My *Voice of Slow* had a chance to show itself and it was welcomed.

- Do you give yourself time and space to hear your own music?

- If you did, what would it sound like?

- What would it feel like?

- Do you have a sign which represents your music?

Pay attention to the notes

I have an involuntary sign that my hand and arm make, almost of their own accord, from time to time (it has long been known that I am a bit weird!) It is a sign that has been in my life for years, which I know represents my music. The music inside of me. It is like a gentle flow. The sound of my sign is like a harp playing.

This flowing sign is how I recognise when something is right. It is a sign which indicates my music is turned on.

- If you could hear your music what sign would it have?

- And what kind of sound?

Listen to the sound of your own music inside – it has a message for you every time it plays.

Talking too much

There is a time to talk and a time to be silent. It is important to be aware of the impact of your chatter on yourself and on others. I have had periods in my life when I have talked too much, exhausting both myself and those around me (sorry!) Nowadays, I am more able to keep silent. I get more pleasure from listening and can now stand back more than I used to.

A friend of mine can talk. He is a very clever, kind and funny guy, but when he talks, he goes at such a rate that you soon find yourself struggling to keep up. When you answer one question, he goes off on another tangent and so on which becomes harder and harder to follow. I don't think he is aware of how fast he speaks and how much he jumps around in conversations. Can he be silent? He does like his own company and often goes off on long walks and runs, so despite the pace of his conversation, it seems he can also turn it off when required.

The Power of Silence

There is a great power in silence. I can feel it in my home as I write this. I feel it in the early mornings when I am out walking. I relish it at night time, whilst lying in the dark, feeling the peaceful presence of silence.

Just take a moment to turn off all the noise around you. Take a deep breath and listen to the silence around you. As you notice your breathing, feel the power in the silence around you.

Time to think and hear yourself

We all need time to think and time to be heard.

Laurelle, who I would describe as my spiritual coach as well as being a great friend, has helped me to hear myself. I am so grateful for this. I have a session with her about once every six weeks.

She not only gives me time to think, she gives me space to hear myself. The ability to do this is extremely valuable. We all need to learn to do this for ourselves, but this does take practice.

Giving yourself time to be silent by turning off all stimulants and distractions is a good start. Five minutes to start with is enough. You can increase this time as you become more able to just to be silent. The more you practise it, the easier and more enjoyable it will become.

Your music is always there

Your music is always there – you just need the space to hear it. As I have explained, I felt that I had lost mine before I went walking my Caminos. I had been too busy, carrying too much, doing too much, and was involved in some work situations which had stopped giving me joy. I needed to change but was finding it hard. I was aware of my music, but it was playing so softly that I could hardly hear it.

As I walked the many miles of the Camino, I kept being shown signs that let me know that my music needed to be expressed. On one particular day, I remember noticing a light by my bedside in one of the guest house rooms in Portugal. It was a bulb set in a birdcage. I reflected on how much at the time, I felt like that light. It burned so brightly yet it was behind bars and could only show itself in parts. I felt sad as I looked at it. I wanted to open the door of the cage and let the light out as if it was a bird that needed to be set free to fly.

Maybe your music has been in a cage and it is time to let it out now?

I have been aware of my light getting brighter the minute I started to follow my *Voice of Slow*.

Everyone has a light inside themselves – it just needs turning on.

Life can create the space for you to hear your music

I have noticed that life does have a habit of creating space for you to make much-needed changes. Something may happen that you are not expecting, which may seem bad at the time, but when you stand back and look at the bigger picture, turns out to have been a blessing in disguise.

Matt used to be a high earner in the City, then very suddenly out of the blue he was made redundant. He tried to get back into a similar job but after about 12 months of trying, with his redundancy package rapidly running out, he had to start thinking about doing something different. He had always loved writing, liked meeting people, and had a burning passion for learning about the world around him. His music was in his ability to find information and turn it into creatively-written pieces which would appeal to readers.

The space he was given after his redundancy gave him time to think about what he would really want to do with his life. He is now a freelance writer and writes books, marketing, PR and editorial content. He loves what he does. He doesn't make as much money as he did when he was a City analyst, but he is rich in self-expression and in enthusiasm for what he does. Had he not been made redundant he might not have allowed himself the luxury of time out to think about himself, and may not have ended up changing his path. The journey for him has not been easy, as this choice carried with it feelings of guilt and failure. However, three years on, he now feels he has something which he can be proud of and is so much more fulfilled than had he stayed on in the City.

Are you aware of times in your life when things have gone wrong, but in going wrong, they have managed to prompt or create a much-needed change in your life?

I had a similar situation myself, when a very good grant for business coaching which I had come to rely upon was suddenly pulled by the government without any warning. This impacted a number of the client contracts which I'd already lined up for the year ahead and created a huge void in my workflow. I had been feeling extremely overloaded with the intensity of these coaching sessions but, at the same time, I was so grateful for the guaranteed supply of work. However not having this grant and the associated work did create the space which I so desperately needed to hear my own music again! I have since made some positive changes to my work which might not have happened if this grant had still been available.

Out of Darkness comes Light

You may relate to these experiences. Sometimes things must go badly wrong before they go right. It may be your *Voice of Slow's* way of getting your attention. It may be telling you that there is important change on its way.

Listen to Your Life

I always think that there is so much to be learnt daily from our own lives. There are so many things to pay attention to when you give yourself space to do so. If you do slow down, you will see things which you may have missed before. Most importantly you will hear yourself.

When you listen to your *Voice of Slow* and what it has to say to you, it will remind you of your music, music you were born to share.

Dare to dream

What makes you happy? Really happy? What would you do with your life right now if you had free choice? What do you dream of in those quieter moments? Are your dreams about things, or are they about experiences and having the freedom to enjoy them?

Notice what you dream about.

Being true to yourself in life is so important. Living your life on your terms. We all change over time and what we want can also change as we evolve and grow.

Values

What is important to you at present in your life? Really important?

What do you really value? And are you living a life that is enabling you to be true to your values? Family, relationships, freedom, fun, travel, nature, health, security, learning, challenge, peace – are your values alive throughout your life?

If not, what do you really want? What would transform your life and make it one which you would be truly excited and grateful to be living?

Being true to YOU

Can you be yourself and still be successful? Is that what we all really want? To feel that we are living a good life, one which is true to our own calling. We all want to feel successful according to our own definition of 'success', whilst being at peace with ourselves and comfortable in our own skin. I was going to write a book with that title when I was 32 years old. I wondered back then if I could be myself and still be successful? I didn't write that book, but it has been one of the constant themes in my life.

Can I be myself? Yes, I can. Can you? Yes, you can. Am I enough as myself? Yes, I am. Are you? Yes, you are!

Reflections from the *Voice of Slow*:

During this section allow your *Voice of Slow* to come forward.

The *Voice of Slow* wants the best for you. It knows you are enough, just as you are. Listen to this gentle voice and trust in its intentions.

Being able to sing the song you came here to sing in this life is a blessing. You are never too old to start something new and be true to yourself.

Your *Voice of Slow* may have the answers to the questions below:

Reflections

What have you found the hardest in your life, yet learnt the most from?

What do you think that you were born to learn in life?

What are you really good at?

What gives you most joy?

If you could live your dream, what would it be?

You are more powerful than you think you are. When you connect to the energy of your *Voice of Slow*, you will be able to take the steps towards realising your dreams.

12. Creating Flow

"When you realise that there is nothing lacking, the whole world belongs to you"

Lao Tzu

This chapter is all about what we can do to **attract flow** in our life once we have found our way.

Flow usually comes when we are following our music, our values, and being true to our authentic selves.

Flow in life can sometimes get blocked when we race through life at breakneck speed. This is all about finding ways to release this vital energy force to enable us to live to our fullest potential.

Ask yourself

- Is your life flowing in the way you want it?

- Does any part of your life feel blocked?

- What is flow?

Creating Flow

You will recognise *'flow'* in business, in your job or personal life – it is when everything seems easy and effortless. You feel completely natural, as if you are meant to be doing exactly what you are doing. You are using your talents and skills to the full and are feel good about yourself. It is as if the pieces of the jigsaw just fall into place. Opportunities come your way and there seems to be no resistance or blockage. Your river is running freely. It is a beautiful feeling.

Flow can also be personal, coming to you at various moments. You may be doing something creative when suddenly, all your brilliance just seems to pour out of you. You may be doing something physical after months of training and then it all comes together and you are amazing. You may be speaking to an audience about something you are passionate about, and it feels like you are just channelling something beautiful right through you.

I have had moments like this in my life. Have you?

Flow can also occur when the circumstances all align to bring about the realisation of your dreams, goals, and ambitions. Flow is when it works. There may be blockages, but the strength of flow finds its way around them. There is movement, process, energy, and excitement.

Have you experienced this at times in your life?

It is as important to recognise when you are in flow, as to understand when you are not. Flow can become blocked when you are out of alignment with yourself, when you are trying to follow a path which is not right for you, trying to push yourself in a direction that you should not be going in. I have talked about this in previous chapters.

Understanding flow from nature

It is useful to think about flow from a different perspective, that of nature.

Many rivers start from a spring high up in the mountains, fed by glacial snow. Water always flows downhill, growing in size and volume, from a small stream to a mighty river.

No matter where or how they start, all rivers ultimately travel in the same direction, out towards the sea. The river looks after itself, changing its direction from time to time, meandering, washing plants and soil from the land into their waters. These contain the nutrients needed for life to survive in the river.

The consistent flow

If you watch the flow of a river, it is constant. It keeps on moving. Yet it is peaceful to watch, passing over rocks, polishing and smoothing them as it goes. The river sometimes needs to increase its energy, when flowing through rapids or waterfalls. It even flows underground from time to time – that's the part you can't see. The only blocks to the river's natural flow are man-made interventions. Left to its own devices, the river keeps going, day after day, always renewing and making its way onwards.

Think about your life flowing like a river.

Flow at a consistent pace, don't intervene with self-inflicted pressure. Allow yourself to meander from time to time to gather the nutrients you need to replenish and look after yourself.

Flow past the boulders and cascade over the rapids, smoothing out the stones as you go.

Always travel forwards, moving peacefully.

There are answers to our question about flow in the way a river runs.

What creates flow?

When I walked the Caminos, I often found myself following mountain streams. I used to watch the water flowing in just the way I have described and used to imagine my own life flowing like a stream. At the time, I wanted more flow. I thought about the dams, and the boulders, and the blockages and why I always seemed to be coming up against them when all I wanted to do was flow.

There were aspects of my business life which I knew were not right, things that I was not happy with. I was aware of a lack of alignment when I was working with on a business project with two business colleagues. We wanted different things. We were all talented people, but there was a lack of chemistry between us. There was no flow. But I didn't know what to do to unblock the dam. It was affecting me.

Why do things get blocked?

I am sure you must have felt *'blocked'* in your life at some time. There may have been times when everything seemed to be a struggle, when there seemed to be no flow at all. Times like this do pass. It may be that you just need to be patient and not to give up, or it may be that you need to change your direction.

Things get blocked when we have lessons to learn. I have learnt my biggest lessons in life from the boulders or the dams which have blocked my path. I have learnt how to navigate them and how to continue to flow forward. The blocks come from a misalignment of some nature, a lack of clarity.

My best friend, Carla, was living a life which seemed to have been blocked for a long time. Living unhappily with a partner on a remote farm, coping with his mystery long-term illness, dealing with his family problems alongside her own personal struggles from letting go of her career and her independence. She hadn't wanted to be in the position she was in for a long time, but didn't seem to able to do anything to change it. She had lost her vitality, energy and confidence. She talked about what was wrong but didn't really know what she wanted or what was 'right'. She was blocked, stuck, rooted to the spot. I could only listen and support her wherever possible, which made me feel useless at times. I wanted her to be happy more than anything, but it seemed that both she and her partner were blocked.

One day she said to me she was tired of fighting her life and was just going to go with it. She surrendered to her situation and stopped pushing herself to make changes. Over time she has found peace and learnt to be grateful for what she does have. She has been patient. Her partner is now much better, and is kind and supportive of her. She takes one day at a time and lives for the present. Her life has more flow now. She has navigated the boulders but not changed her course. She tells me that she has learnt a lot about relationships from this experience.

So, flow does not mean that things have to suddenly become amazing. A quiet sense of peace and joy in where you are and with what you have is often more than enough.

Resetting yourself for Flow

Flow can become blocked by negative energy. This can be caused by many different elements which are often outside of our consciousness; things connected with our life experiences (both past and present), with our deeper way of thinking, and with the people and circumstances which we have attracted into our lives. Language and behaviour can reveal a lot about what is going on with us, on the inside. I remember once describing the process of moving a business forward like a fight. A fight requires a great deal of effort – it is different from flow. A flow suggests an easiness and feeling of pleasure. Many people would like more of a flow of money in their life, but at the same time complain about the lack of it.

Flow 'From' and 'To' Abundance

Flow comes from a place of abundance (think back to the image of flowing water) and can be blocked by messages of lack. If you want more flow, you first need to look at what you already have and be grateful for it. This creates a positive energy which attracts flow and starts to get it moving. You may say that if you haven't got any money, how can you see abundance?

However, the point is that you do have abundance in other areas of your life. There is always an abundance of silence, of peace, of beauty in nature, of rivers and streams flowing, of sunshine and rain. Just imagine that you have that flow with your money. Connect it to nature. Be thankful for the abundance that you already have and reset your financial radar to one of flow.

If you want more flow, watch your language and make sure you feed your brain the right messages. If you focus on lack, you tend to attract more, yet if you focus on what you already have and imagine the abundance of more, it switches the focus to the right channel.

This is why, when you connect with your talents and strengths and spend time doing what you are good at, flow seems to happen much more easily. Playing to your strengths in a team and respecting one another for your respective contributions can also be a great way of transforming the energy and flow of a business. This is one of the lessons which the management team for our business network needed to learn. We are all different people, and all great at managing and leading specific areas. Allowing each other to be amazing and letting go of the reins of control long enough to allow everyone's light to shine enables the necessary energy to navigate and flow past the boulders. It is just a matter of understanding that flow goes where energy leads. Recapture the energy and the flow will take care of itself.

Reflections from the *Voice of Slow*

During this section allow your *Voice of Slow* to come forward.

The *Voice of Slow* wants the best for you. It knows you are enough, just as you are. Listen to this gentle voice and trust in its intentions.

Once you get flow in your life, you will feel it. Things will feel easier, like they are meant to be. You will feel the cloud lift and the sun come out. You have the power to remove the blocks and allow flow.

Reflections

Where do you feel blocked in your life?

How would you describe the flow you want?

What could unblock the energy?

What could allow the flow to navigate the boulders?

What language and visualisation could help?

If you want more flow in your life, work on your alignment and clarity first. Make sure that your purpose is aligned with your values and you are using your greatest talents and strengths for what you do.

13. Creating Energy with Slow

"There are many ways of going forwards but only one way of standing still"

This chapter is all about how **taking time** to slow down is also about creating energy. Slowing down can enable you to accomplish more.

When you slow down you are able to pay more attention to how you are treating your body, mind and spirit.

It is so important to look after yourself and remember you are not a machine. You need your energy to enable you to live your life to its full potential.

Ask yourself

- Have you noticed the ebb and flow of your own energy?

- Do you have peaks and troughs in your day?

- Do your energy levels affect your mood and what you are able to accomplish at any given time?

The ebb and flow of our energy

Energy is vital to us all. With it, we can access our greatness. We are our most valuable asset.

Energy is life. The life and Soul inside us all. To feel good, we need to be able to access that energy. If you treat your body like a machine, expecting it to go on performing without regular care and attention, it will let you down at some point and you will become ill. Without your health, your life would be very different indeed. We all tend to take our health for granted; that is until something goes wrong.

Stress can make you sick

Falling ill can be a way of forcing us to slow down, to make changes, and to look after ourselves better. In my experience, it is better to take steps to prevent falling ill, rather than waiting until you receive a wake-up call. Having said that, I too have had my fair share of wake-up calls. I was lucky to have had a wake-up call early in my life, having been diagnosed with breast cancer when I was only 31 years old. Luckily it was only Grade One and I recovered quickly without any relapses. Still I had to deal with those fateful words, "I am sorry but the lump is cancerous". I can remember to this day, arguing with the doctor who told me, telling her that it simply couldn't be possible.

Sadly, it was, and I had to face it.

Why did I get breast cancer? I do believe in the connection between the mind, body, and spirit. I think that the number of what I would call *'nest traumas'* which I had undergone up to that age may have been a significant factor. From a very young age, I had lived with the fear of my parents splitting up (which they did when I was a teenager), in my late 20's I suffered a breakdown in my own marriage (which had only lasted a year), and at the time of my cancer diagnosis, I was going through a very challenging relationship with someone who kept letting me down (with whom I split up soon after). So, at the time, I didn't feel good in my own skin, and knew something was wrong. It was and it came out physically.

When I was in hospital I met a number of women who also had breast cancer; most of them had had some sort of stressful time leading up to their diagnosis. This is not always the case of course, but a stressful life and an illness are often connected.

My brush with breast cancer took me a while to get over, but it did make me aware that, despite my attitude of 'I-don't-do-illness', I became ill when I was vulnerable. I have always taken great care since, and I urge you to do the same. I recall feeling a powerful presence as I was undergoing this experience. I felt a sense of peace and knew, deep down, that everything was ok. I was grateful for the feeling that someone or something was with me at the time – it was very comforting to feel like I was being looked after. It gave me the strength to deal with everything.

Your *Voice of Slow* wants the best for you

Your *Voice of Slow* wants you to access a powerful source of infinite energy; it wants you to feel vital and connected with that source.

If I asked you – 'What energy do you want, and when do you want it?' – what would your answer be? You might reply, 'I want to jump out of bed feeling great, to feel like I can keep going all day, making lots of important decisions, to be able to finish all my tasks, to go to the gym on my way home, and still have the energy to cook dinner and spend time with my kids.'

That might be a tall order and the reality is that we all expect a lot of ourselves. If you made a list of all things you expected yourself to accomplish in a typical day and read it back to yourself, I am sure it would be very comprehensive! Did you undertake it with maximum energy and enthusiasm at all times? I expect not. Did you feel tired at different times of the day? Probably. And most importantly what did you do to take care of yourself?

The importance of looking after your mind and body

I work with business owners, professionals, and directors who always have a lot to do. It is a huge challenge to grow a small business, with many owner managers ending up doing an awful lot themselves, working long hours, weekends, and finding it hard to take time for holidays. They fail to appreciate that they are their business' greatest asset and that they too need taking care of. If they fell ill, what would happen to the business? Many say that they haven't got time to be ill. They can't slow down, as if they did, nothing would ever get done.

How well do things actually get done if you are tired and stressed? Not as well as they could, I'm sure.

When I walked my Caminos, the most important thing I learnt to take care of was my feet. When I didn't, I suffered from awful blisters which became very painful and made it almost impossible to continue. So, I had to stop walking on occasions. I learnt that it was better to prepare and take care. It is the same in life – it is better to manage your energy than to just go full bore until you burn out.

Work-life balance

Speeding through life without awareness can take its toll on your work-life balance. Work – Eat – Sleep – Repeat is not good! There needs to be a balance. But why do we sometimes not give ourselves the care and attention we require? Why do we put ourselves and our needs at the bottom of any Priority List? Most people want – and would value – more energy, but can feel blocked when it comes to making the necessary changes. The old excuses of, 'I haven't got time', or 'I am too busy', spring to mind.

Your *Voice of Slow* wants you to spend time enriching your Soul with the things that feed your energy. It wants the best for you, but do you heed its call?

So, what feeds your energy. What do you love doing? Are you doing enough of it?

I love the things which I can do physically – walking, running, riding, cycling – and know that I am blessed to be able to. In fact, I am physically fitter now than I was in my 30s. I almost wish I had realised the pleasure of some of these activities when I was younger and then I would have had longer doing them. I get a lot of energy from exercise and make sure I prioritise time to do it every day.

What to do to access an abundance of energy

There are things you can do to ensure you do leap out of bed with a spring in your step, to give of your best to your work, to have enough energy for those people that are important to you in your life and to sleep well at night. These things may involve changing some habits and if the desire is there to feel good, they are changes worth making, aren't they?

Moving your body

It can be too easy to live a sedentary life, drive a car, take a bus, the lift, the escalator, or to sit at our computers. Technology has transformed the way that we move and communicate. It is easy not to move much. And if you don't move your body, it becomes lazy and tired. So you put on weight and it gets even heavier to move. The less you move, the less you want to.

Exercise releases endorphins which make us feel good. It also makes us feel physically fitter and more able to deal with our daily tasks. It will help your brain work better; you will be sharper and able to think more clearly. I wouldn't be without my 30-minute run or 60-minute walk in the morning before work, even if I have to walk to a meeting or get up earlier to do my exercise. I notice that I am definitely more switched on when I have had some fresh air. I need it.

I also find that I can do some great creative thinking when I am out running, walking, or riding my old horse, Magic. I can think through any challenges, come up with ideas and think about my vision. I also practice my presentations or talks whilst I ride or walk – I just have to make sure nobody is about! It is lovely to do that with the wind in my hair and being out in nature. It is such a great way to start the day.

Walking can help you recover

Walking can help you to feel better when you are feeling stressed or overloaded. Our physiology influences how we feel.

Notice what you look like and how you move when you are feeling down. The chances are you will be looking down, shoulders hunched, moving slowly, with an expression on your face that expresses the load you are carrying. You may not be able to change how you feel, but you can change how you move. If you go for a short brisk walk, shoulders back and looking up, your body will send a message back to your brain, I am ok! This really does help maintain your health in tough times.

I did a lot of this during very tough periods in my life, getting over breakups, coping with the grief of losing loved ones, dealing with conflict and stress at work. I have walked miles and miles over the years walking through my pain. It has helped me to recover and to maintain my health during periods of high stress.

What can you do for yourself?

What do you do for exercise? What would you like to do?

It doesn't have to be much to make a big difference. A simple 20 to 30-minute brisk walk will make a massive difference to your energy levels. Movement, no matter how small over time, will build up and ensure a positive impact. It is one of those things that you don't know how wonderful it could be if you don't give it a go.

My advice would be to find something you can enjoy and just take the first step. It could be a dance class, the gym, badminton, tennis, walking, golf, or cycling. If you find it hard to do it alone, find a buddy. When I started running I used to have a friend call round in the mornings to make me do it. It was hard to start with but now I can run a half marathon. Just take the first steps and you could be amazed at where they lead you.

Water of life

It is important to stay hydrated – drinking enough fresh water will ensure you do. Do you drink enough? Tea and coffee don't count apparently (I always thought green tea did!) Think about it like this, if you want more positive flow in your life. Water flows, so why not fill your body with it? This how I remind myself of the importance of water in my life. Drinking enough water daily, like all the other things that are good for your health, needs to become a habit. The recommended amount of water is 2 litres a day, so water really does need to be your daily companion. Do you notice when you are feeling dehydrated? This will affect your energy levels. Drink a pint of water and notice how you feel. Go on, get one right now while you read this. Think as you are drinking it, how much it is giving you. Say thank you. Water is free, it is abundantly available and it does you good.

Look after what you put into your body

We have all been blessed with a body to live our lives through. Our body needs us to look after it. What we choose to put into it will affect its ability to look and feel good. Good nutrition is vital and it affects the energy our bodies are able to draw upon. It is so easy to grab a chocolate bar, for the sugar rush mid-afternoon when you feel your energy dip and to eat processed or fast foods when you are in a hurry, but in the long-term, that is like putting the wrong oil in your car – eventually, it will affect its power. This is not a book about healthy eating but it is about the *Voice of Slow*. If you slow down and pay attention to what you are putting into your body, you will give yourself a chance to decide what is really going to be good for you.

We all know that good nutrition has a huge impact on your energy levels, but do we give ourselves time to give this enough attention? If you eat a healthy breakfast at the start of your day (in my case I may choose porridge, fruit and yoghurt), I can feel the slow energy release and know how long it will keep me going. Having something healthy pre-prepared for lunch is also a good idea if you know you are going to be on the go all day and are likely to otherwise grab something unhealthy.

Eating early enough in the evening to allow at least three hours before you go to bed is also good for you, as it means you don't go to bed on a full stomach. It also means you create a period of fasting time overnight. If you eat your last meal at 7pm, go to bed at 10.30pm and have breakfast at 7.30am – it gives you a full 12 hours without food, which also has health benefits.

What you put in you get out

Being mindful of what you are putting into your body each day and what you are expecting of it, is important. If you wanted to run a marathon you would need the right fuel. It is the same whatever you are doing each day. I always feel grateful to have the body I have (I admit, maybe I do catch myself complaining sometimes). OK, so it doesn't look as good as it did when I was younger but it is still in good shape. It's not perfect but it is healthy and I can do most things easily. I do look after it better now than I did when I was younger, it is more important as the years pass by. So, do think about what you can do to ensure your body gets the good nutrition and the care it needs to help you get the most out of your days.

Sleep

How many hours of sleep do you need to feel good? The recommended eight hours may seem a lot, but actually our bodies need it to function at their best. I find I can operate quite well on less sleep: six to eight hours depending on what I am doing. You need to find what works for you. I find that my working body clock is changing from one that used to operate at it best late into the night when everything was quiet to one that is better early in the morning. I am starting to make the most of the early morning energy and peace, which I can only benefit from if I get up at 5 or 6am. To do this I need to get to bed earlier. It is a habitual pattern I am working on, and, so far, I am seeing the benefits when I do achieve it. It is so great to have spent two hours writing and have had an hour of exercise and fresh air before I start my 'proper work' at 9 am.

If, for whatever reason, you have trouble getting to sleep, I would recommend creating a period of downtime before you go to bed. You should ideally have a few hours before going to bed when you are not looking at technology (and that means, don't take your phone or iPad to bed with you!) Read a book, have a relaxing bath, listen to music, do some meditation or whatever else that relaxes you. Expecting just to close your eyes and have a relaxing night's sleep when you have a head filled with the stuff of the day is asking a lot of your body. Give it a chance to wind down and chill out, and you will feel the benefit.

Time out to reflect

We all need thinking time or space to ponder our issues, dilemmas, and decisions. I find that I think so much more clearly when I am walking or riding my old horse out in the countryside. In fact, taking time to do that is actually an investment in the health of my business and my personal life. The problems I solve and the ideas I have are of a much higher quality than those I have when sat in front of my PC, on the phone, or in meetings.

Clarity

Slowing down and giving yourself the headspace you need to think clearly is vital. Rushing and doing things too quickly can often waste more time in the end, especially if you have to redo the things that did not turn out quite as you expected. Here is a good example of that. I recently rushed the production of some training material because I thought I knew it well enough and could deliver it easily. As soon as I went through a practice run I realised that it just was not good enough and I had to go back to the drawing board and rethink everything. I was annoyed with myself for trying to rush something so important and not giving it the time it deserved. There are times when going slower and giving yourself time will ultimately pay greater dividends. You may have had your own experiences of this.

Meditation

Learn how to meditate so that you can give yourself time during a busy day to connect with yourself inside.

It doesn't have to take long - just 20 minutes a day will have a powerful impact on your well-being, clarity of thinking, and feeling of personal power inside. I give myself time in the evening as I find this is when it is easiest for me to shut down the outside and go inside. I have created a nice quiet space in my home to meditate, with some special objects which contribute to the energy and atmosphere; a candle, my quartz crystal, and my peace heart.

To prevent myself falling asleep, I sit up straight on my small comfortable couch. I either listen to a guided meditation, gentle music, or simply sit in silence and focus on my breathing, letting the thoughts that enter my mind drift away in clouds. This is a very simple practice that I do daily. I look forward to it at the end of the day – it is part of my 'letting-go' routine.

There are no rules for meditation. You can do it whenever is best for you in your day. It can be five minutes or longer. It just depends on your lifestyle and what you want out of it. Sometimes it can be good to join a group, both to learn to meditate and to maintain the practice. I am blessed to have a wonderful teacher who leads a monthly group. This practice has given me so much joy and peace, reminding me who I really am inside. The regular practice of meditation will help to keep you strong and resilient in the face of all the things life brings up for you to deal with.

Reflections from the *Voice of Slow*

During this section allow your Voice of Slow to come forward.

The *Voice of Slow* wants the best for you. It knows you are enough, just as you are. Listen to this gentle voice and trust in its intentions.

Slow can enable you to create energy, the energy you need to thrive. Your work-life balance is important.

Reflections

What does your *Voice of Slow* want for your work-life balance?

What could you stop doing?

What could you start doing?

Mini meditation

Imagine a peaceful place that you could go to whenever you needed to just be with yourself. It could be in the countryside, by the sea, beside a flowing stream or sitting on a hill in the sunshine, anywhere where you know you feel good. Close your eyes and just imagine being there. Make a big screen in your mind's eye and just watch it as if it was a movie. This is a very easy meditative practice and you can go there whenever you just need a moment of peace and joy in your busy day.

Energy creator

Our bodies and our Souls need energy to thrive. Imagine yourself like a tree with roots at your feet reaching deep down, connecting with the energy of the earth, your arms reaching upwards like branches to the sky connecting with the vast universal energy above you. Look up and imagine this energy following through you from the ground beneath your feet to the sky above your head. It is a wonderful feeling and will bring you energy whenever you need it.

INDEX

EPILOGUE

The Gift of Slow

Your *Voice of Slow* wants the best for you. It wants you to be happy and fulfilled. It wants you to see clearly, connect with your deepest yearning and to fulfil what you came here to do. We all have our own routes to walk in life, have experiences that will enable us as unique individuals to learn the lessons meant just for us.

Your *Voice of Slow* wants to be heard. It needs you to give it space, time, and attention, to reflect on and to take heed of what it has to say to you. When you do this, you will feel the joy that was always meant for you to have, a joy that is freely available to access whenever you need it. The *Voice of Slow* is always there for you. You are never alone.

Message for you from me

I have loved writing this book, it has been my joy. As I said at the beginning, writing it has been as much for me as it has been for you. I, like you, am in *Pursuit of Slow* and this is only the starting point. I really needed to hear my *Voice of Slow*, but I didn't know it until I first heard its voice whilst walking the Camino de Santiago de Compostela.

I now give my *Voice of Slow* daily reflection time and, as a result, I learn something new every day that helps me in my personal journey. I am now enjoying more flow, ease, and meaningful abundance in my life for which I am truly grateful. I feel I am on the right track now and can both walk and run forward. I feel stronger and more at peace with myself than I have in many years. Most importantly I feel more trust in my path.

I want the same for you.

Sharing these powerful messages, insights and learning is my way of giving. We are all the same at a deeper level and I know what I am saying will resonate with everyone who reads this. Your *Voice of Slow* is you, the real you, the you that knows what is best and will always be there.

More help

If you have enjoyed reading this book and wish to continue a connection with your *Voice of Slow,* here are some more options for you (after you've written a review of the book, of course):

- Join the '*In Pursuit of Slow Community*' and gain access to practical tools, inspiration and support for your journey at inpursuitofslow.com

- Follow the Voice of Slow on Twitter at @inpursuitofslow

- If you are a business owner who feels a need to slow down to gain more clarity and would value support and guidance to do that, please go to my website www.jackiejarvis.co.uk for information about my individual and team coaching plus mastermind group options for help.

- An inspiring speaker for your conference or event – *Slow Down to Gain More, with important messages from the Voice of Slow for Life and Business.* More details at inpursuitofslow.com/public-speaking

The *'Voice of Slow'* at Conferences and Events

Lynn Shepherd, Executive Chair of Venturefest Oxford, Co-Founder of TECH-Tonic

"Jackie was a guest speaker at our TECHTonic network meeting – a forum for the women of Oxfordshire working in tech to collaborate and support each other. She talked about the *'Voice of Slow'* and as women, we all 'got it'! There seemed to be an audible intake of breath as Jackie's message to slow down and be more successful hit home. Our talk lasted over an hour, such were the questions and conversations that followed. Read the book, listen to her talk – it will change how you think and how you act!"

Nikki Poole – Managing Director Hedges Law

"Jackie was a guest speaker at our Salus Women Charity event – an event for women to raise money for the refurbishment of the breast cancer unit at the Churchill hospital in Oxford. You could have heard a pin drop as she spoke about the *Voice of Slow*; everyone related to it. The creative way in which she told the story of her Camino de Santiago adventure to bring the *Voice of Slow* alive was brilliant. We were all engaged by it."

Sylvia Baldock – Professional Speaker, Coach, Trainer, Author

"I have heard Jackie speak a number of times about her experience walking the Camino de Santiago de Compostela when she first heard the *Voice of Slow*. I found her mesmerising on stage and her messages extremely powerful. Slowing down and letting go of that which no longer serves us has a truth in it for all of us. Looking after our own well-being is essential for success in business."

Jeremy Nicholas – President PSA London

"Jackie's *Voice of Slow* talk at the Professional Speaking Association in London was brilliant. I loved the way she used her heavy rucksack to represent the burden we all carry. It gave us all a lot to think about."

Fiona Armitage – Partner, Critchleys HR and Payroll

"I saw Jackie speak at a business well-being event about the *Voice of Slow*. I instantly related to her message about the impact of overload and the power of letting go of the things that were no longer serving me. As a business owner, I can be guilty of working very hard and being very busy, but not always accomplishing what is most important. Jackie's talk really made be stop and think, not just about my business but my personal life too. I now go out on my bike more often."

Michelle Mills-Porter – MD Ethos Development Ltd

"I booked Jackie to speak to our PSA Midlands group after seeing her speak several times. I feel she has a really strong message. I loved the authentic way she told her story which helped us all connect with our own *Voice of Slow*. This particularly resonated with me as I find it hard to slow down and I know it is important for my own health and well-being."

Rachel McGuinness – Chief Vitality Officer – Wake up with Zest

"I saw Jackie speak at a health and well-being event about the *Voice of Slow*. It was really captivating. As a health and well-being expert myself, and as someone who has suffered burnout in the past, I totally related to her powerful messages. Mental, physical, and emotional well – being is vital to success in business and happiness in life. We all need to do what we can to look after ourselves."

You can contact me personally at jackie@jackiejarvis.co.uk

I look forward to continuing our journey together.

With much love,

Jackie

ACKNOWLEDGEMENTS

I am so very grateful for all the help, support, and encouragement I have received. I would like to thank the following people for their valuable contributions:

Matt Wright for his careful, detailed editing and proofreading of my work, whilst maintaining its authentic voice

David Harris for his work bringing the *Voice of Slow* alive in the digital world and enabling us to connect with a worldwide audience

Sylvia Baldock for her speaker coaching which has given me the confidence and skill to get on stage to share these powerful *Voice of Slow* messages as an inspirational speaker.

Laurelle Rond for her wonderful meditation, chanting, and sound therapy sessions which have worked their magic for me over many years.

My life experiences with all the ups and downs, good times and bad, for without them I would not be here now, having finished this book, and able to share these important lessons with you.

With Love,

Jackie

InPursuitOfSlow.com